THE ENGLISH LAKES

The English Lakes

TEXT BY
Robin Whiteman

PHOTOGRAPHS BY
Rob Talbot

Weidenfeld & Nicolson
London

First published in 1989 by George Weidenfeld & Nicolson Ltd,
91 Clapham High Street, London SW4 7TA

Half-title page: Grasmere Island, Grasmere
Title page: Ullswater, from Gowbarrow Park

Contents

ACKNOWLEDGEMENTS

Robin Whiteman and Rob Talbot would like to thank everyone who so willingly gave their time to guide them around the properties and sites. They particularly wish to acknowledge the generous co-operation they received from the National Trust (North West Region).

They are also grateful to the following: Mr & Mrs Hal Bagot, Levens Hall, who were especially kind and helpful, and to Mr T. Schofield for his help with the interior photography; Mrs M. Henderson (owner of Rydal Mount) with particular thanks to Don Brookes (Curator of Rydal Mount); Mr and Mrs Patrick Gordon-Duff-Pennington of Muncaster Castle; Dr Terry McCormick (Resident Curator) and Rosemary Hoggarth (Photographic Unit) of The Wordsworth Trust; Reverend K. E. Wood, St Oswald's Church, Grasmere; Colin Saxton for his enthusiastic support; Bryn Hughes for his useful information on Honister Quarry; Craig Murchie for his invaluable knowledge of the mountains; and Mr and Mrs Danny Birkett of Yew Tree Farm, Coniston, who were extremely helpful and accommodating.

Special thanks go to Trisha, Sheila and Anne for all their support and encouragement. Appreciation goes also to all those individuals and organizations too numerous to mention by name who nevertheless made such a valuable contribution.

THE LAKE DISTRICT

General map of the area showing some of the locations illustrated in this book.

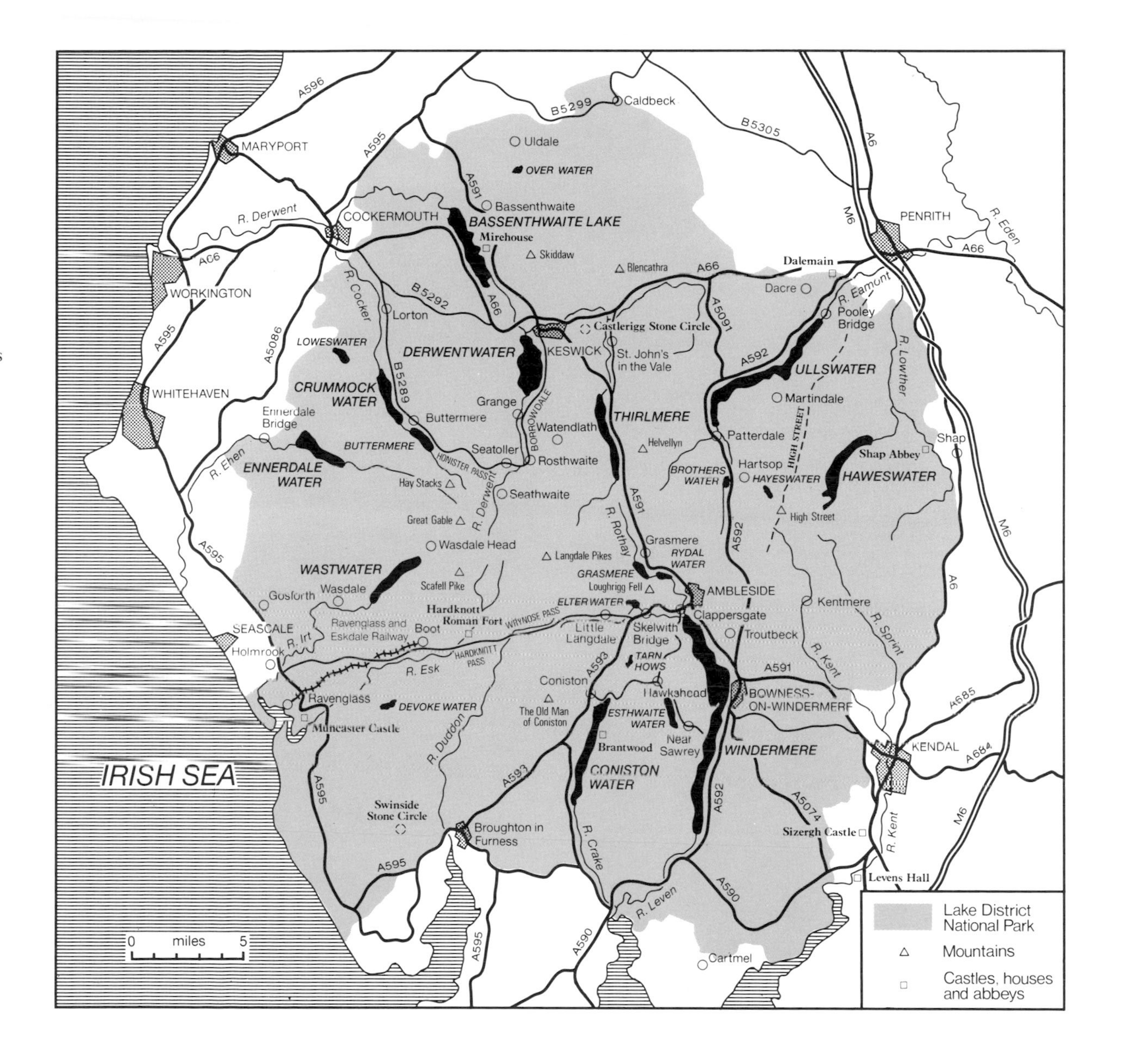

INTRODUCTION

RYDAL WATER

This lovely reed-edged lake, just three-quarters of a mile long, a quarter of a mile wide and only 56 feet deep at its deepest point, lies in the valley of the River Rothay between Ambleside and Grasmere. It takes its name from Rydal village, situated at its eastern end, but was originally known as Routhermere or Rothaymere after the river. The lake is sheltered by Nab Scar to the north and Loughrigg Fell to the south, and, more often than not, the surface of the water is silvery calm with scarcely a ripple to disturb the herons that nest on its two wooded islets. Although renowned for its association with Wordsworth, who lived nearby at Rydal Mount for the last thirty-seven years of his life, it was also the home of Thomas De Quincy and Hartley Coleridge, who both lived for a while at Nab Cottage on the northern shore of the lake. At the edge of the water close to the village is a low rock hidden by trees, known as the Poet's Seat.

Dawn, and from the east a yellow autumnal light filters through the hanging mist, softly illuminating the dappled silvery surface of the peaceful lake. A low and solitary rock pierces the glassy smoothness of the shallows, and standing on it is a heron – patient, motionless, silent as a sentinel – its keen yellow eyes following the movements of an unsuspecting fish, its deadly dagger-sharp bill poised alert and ready to strike. Nearby, but well away from the danger, a small brown trout glides over the gravel bed, heading upstream away from the lake to the clear cold mountain waters of the fast-flowing River Rothay. Hidden by the mist the bracken- and tree-covered fellsides rise abruptly from the valley floor, the meadows and pastures still fresh and green despite the lateness of the year.

In these early hours of the morning, before the calm is shattered by vehicles and visitors, the scene from the shore of Grasmere seems timeless, appearing almost the same as it would have been at the beginning of the nineteenth century, when the Wordsworths came to live in the valley and William's childhood dream was fulfilled . . . paradise was achieved:

> And now 'tis mine, perchance for life, dear Vale,
> Beloved Grasmere (let the Wandering Streams
> Take up, the cloud-capt hills repeat, the Name),
> One of thy lowly Dwellings is my Home.

Wordsworth and his sister Dorothy moved into what is now known as Dove Cottage on 20 December 1799. After a long absence Wordsworth had finally come home to his native Lakeland and it was here at Grasmere and neighbouring Rydal that he was to spend the rest of his long and extremely productive life. Not only was he a poet, one of the greatest and most influential in the English language, and a symbol of the Romantic Movement which swept across Europe in the late eighteenth and early nineteenth centuries, but he was also a landscape designer, gardener, traveller, Distributor of

Stamps for Westmorland and writer of a guide to the Lakes, first published in 1810. The book sold better than his poems and, despite his constant complaints about the increasing number of visitors, in the end he probably did more than anyone else to make the English Lakes as popular as they are today.

Wordsworth was born and bred in the area and – except for the period between leaving to study at Cambridge in 1787 and returning to live at Grasmere in 1799 – he spent much of his time outdoors exploring the fells and dales on foot, often covering distances of over thirty miles a day. More than any other writer, Wordsworth changed the way in which people looked at and felt about the Lakes.

In the early eighteenth century outsiders thought that the region was wild and inhospitable, a horrifying land in which the valleys were too dangerous to enter and the mountains too immense to pass. It seems it was a view that the locals sometimes amused themselves by encouraging, for when Thomas Gray visited the Lakes in 1769 he was solemnly told that desperate men lurked in the distant hills. He ventured nervously part of the way up Borrowdale, terrified that the rocks on either side of the valley would tumble down upon him. When he reached the tiny hamlet of Grange he declined to go any further, convinced that 'all further access is here barred to prying mortals'.

In 1786 William Gilpin published a guide-book entitled *Observations, relative chiefly to Picturesque Beauty, made in the year 1772, on several parts of England; particularly the Mountains and Lakes of Cumberland and Westmorland.* In addition to attracting tourists to the Lakes, his book laid down rules for looking at the landscape. However, as he admitted, these rules very often did not conform with nature: 'I am so attached to my picturesque rules, that if nature goes wrong I cannot help putting her right.'

The picturesque, popularized by Gilpin, meant, quite literally, that the landscape was viewed as if it were a picture. As more and more people read his guide and came to visit the Lakes, this way of seeing hardened into a habit.

In November 1799 Wordsworth, accompanied by Coleridge, went on a 'Pikteresk Toor' of the Lakes, and shortly afterwards he returned to the Lakes permanently. Through his poetry, he broke down the notion of Gilpin's picture frame, seeing the landscape through no one's eyes but his own. Not only did he write about what he saw, but he also expressed what he felt and experienced with a passion so intense that he revolutionized people's perception of the Lakes.

His guide to the Lakes, written in the early nineteenth century, sums up much that he felt about the region and a lot of his fears and observations are, surprisingly, still relevant today.

> I do not know any tract of country in which, within so narrow a compass, may be found an equal variety in the influences of light and shadow upon the sublime or beautiful features of the landscape.

Lakeland, situated in the north-west corner of England, is indeed one of the most beautiful, unspoilt areas in Britain. The variety of landscape crammed into an area only thirty-five miles square is astounding: high peaks, wild fells, spectacular waterfalls, lush pastures, secluded valleys, enchanting lakes, ancient sites, historic buildings, isolated farmsteads, remote villages and bustling towns. It is this extraordinary scenic diversity that makes the region, which encapsulates all that is best in English landscape, so unique. Therein lies its greatest attraction, which acts like a magnet to visitors from all over the world.

It was Wordsworth who first likened the topographical lay-out of the Lakes to an imaginary wheel, with the spokes represented by 'not fewer than eight' valleys radiating out from the central hub of Scafell and Great Gable, though not all contained lakes. In fact, as he was aware, the pattern falls into the shape of two wheels with a second hub on Helvellyn, both wheels being split by a geological fault running north-west to south-east from Thirlmere to Windermere.

To put it more simply, there are three distinct blocks of landscape in the Lakes and each is determined by the rock. In the north the fells – consisting of Skiddaw Slate – are smooth and undulating, dropping steeply and evenly to the valley floors. Skiddaw Slate, one of the oldest rocks on the planet, is a mud-rock formed on the bed of a shallow sea about 500 million years ago.

In the centre are the wild, jagged and irregular peaks of the Borrowdale Volcanics, amongst which is Scafell Pike, at 3,210 feet, the highest mountain in England. This rugged, dramatic landscape – stretching in a broad swath through the middle of Lakeland – was thrown up when the earth erupted in volcanic violence about 450 million years ago. The fine ash that was hurled high into the air fell into shallow water and eventually formed the green slates of Coniston, Honister and elsewhere.

The last of the three main blocks lies to the south, beyond the middle reaches of Coniston Water and Windermere, stretching south-westwards to the Duddon estuary and north-eastwards towards the Pennines. The landscape is gentler and consists mainly of moorland, although in places it is heavily wooded; the hills are more undulating than the northern fells and not as high. The underlying rock was laid down on a sea floor as gritty and muddy sediments during the Silurian age (about 400 million years ago) and weathers easily to form soil.

Between about 350 million years ago and 15 million years ago the earth's surface underwent a series of catastrophic upheavals. The final earth movement, when the mountainous mass around Great Gable and Scafell was thrust upwards into an elongated dome, gave the Lakes their distinctive shape. During the great Ice Ages of the last million years countless glacial movements gouged out the distinctive U-shaped valleys. Following the line of least resistance – the radial pre-glacial valleys cut by rivers – they scoured deep trenches in the valley floors. When the ice finally melted and filled the trenches with water the lakes were formed.

Most authorities agree that there are sixteen lakes while the rest are designated as 'tarns': the largest is Windermere, at over ten miles long, the smallest Elterwater, which is only half a mile long. Not all of them lie on the floor of the glacially eroded valleys. Those that do are usually long and narrow, and surprisingly deep. Wastwater is the deepest, reaching a maximum depth of 258 feet. Other lakes are relatively shallow, like Rydal Water with a maximum depth of 56 feet.

The landscape of the Lakes has undergone enormous changes throughout the immense span of time the earth has been evolving, and it is changing and evolving still: not so dramatically and catastrophically as it has in the past, but subtly, slowly, imperceptibly, day by day and year by year.

The most obvious changes are those that are occurring in the lakes and tarns, all of which are gradually silting up. Buttermere and Crummock Water were once one large lake, and now they are divided by a wide, flat alluvial plain. Derwentwater and Bassenthwaite Lake have been separated in the same way. Numerous tarns have already disappeared and become peat bogs on the fellside. In various other places whole lakes have silted up and vanished – a process which in some cases, notably Kentmere, north of Kendal, has been accelerated by drainage. Elterwater, the smallest of the sixteen lakes, is

TARN HOWS, CONISTON

In addition to the generally accepted sixteen lakes, there are a considerable number of tarns in Lakeland. In his classic study *The Tarns of Lakeland* W. Heaton Cooper features 103 named tarns: there are in fact countless more, and many do not even have names. In 1951 two men from Grasmere, Colin Dodgson and Timothy Tyson, decided to attempt to bathe in every one of Lakeland's tarns. It took the two 'tarn baggers' eight years to complete their task and, in the process, they set a remarkable record, managing to find a total of 463 different tarns. The two men also bathed in a number of dubious tarns, but they were discounted. The highest, at 2,750 feet above sea-level, is Broadcrag Tarn on Scafell Pike. Devoke Water is the largest and is bigger than Elterwater, the smallest lake. Tarn Hows, lying between Hawkshead and Coniston, is by far the most popular, more popular even than any of the lakes. It is also one of the prettiest, possessing not only rocky promontories, tiny islands and wooded shores, but also superb views of the surrounding high fells.

steadily growing smaller as silt deposits build up around its irregular reed-fringed shoreline.

The weather is a major contributing factor in the shifting evolution of the landscape too. Sudden storms – like the one in the summer of 1938 when 9 inches of rain fell in thirty-six hours – can transform a tranquil beck into a raging torrent, bringing tons of soil, stones and boulders down from the fellsides and depositing them thickly on the valley floor. Those rocks that can be readily percolated by water also have a tendency to shatter in the frost, which puts them under enormous pressures. The resulting fragments fall away to create a sloping wall of scree, descending steeply from the high broken crags to the valley floor and, if the valley contains a lake, into the lake itself. The spectacular Wastwater Screes, for example, rises almost 2,000 feet from the floor of the lake to the rugged cliffs of Illgill Head.

Erosion is not only caused by the effects of weathering, however. Since the artists, poets and writers of the late eighteenth century discovered the dramatic and awesome scenery of the English Lakes, millions and millions of visitors have flocked into the region. The sheer weight of their numbers has severely eroded mountain paths and once narrow grassy trails have become eyesores a hundred feet wide.

Wordsworth's guide to the Lakes illustrates that he was aware even then that the increasing number of visitors threatened to destroy the unique character and landscape of the Lakes. In his book he appealed 'that they deem the district a sort of national property, in which every man has a right and interest who has an eye to perceive and a heart to enjoy'. With this enlightening idea that the landscape needed protection, Wordsworth must lay claim to being one of the earliest conservationists. He anticipated the formation of the Lake District National Park in 1951 by over a century. With nearly 900 square miles of Lakeland, it became the largest of ten such parks in Britain, whose aims were to preserve and enhance the natural beauty of an area and promote its enjoyment by the public.

In his 1844 sonnet *On the Projected Kendal and Windermere Railway* Wordsworth protested:

> Is then no nook of English ground secure
> From rash assault?

concluding with a plea that

> . . . if human hearts be dead,
> Speak, passing winds; ye torrents, with your strong
> And constant voice, protest against the wrong.

Wordsworth, however, was not alone in championing the cause of conservation. Others, whose hearts were not dead, took up the challenge, rallying support to preserve the environment from industrial and commercial exploitation while, at the same time, endeavouring to protect the livelihood of the inhabitants and cater for the needs of the ever-increasing flood of visitors.

One of the greatest and most energetic campaigners for the Lakes was Canon Hardwicke Rawnsley, who was vicar of Crosthwaite, Keswick, from 1883 to 1916. Although he took a full and active part in the life of the parish, his other accomplishments were prodigious: he wrote papers on the natural history, literary associations and history of the region and he led the fight against Manchester Corporation's scheme to turn Thirlmere into a reservoir – a battle that was lost. His crowning achievement, however, – for which the nation will always be in his debt – occurred in 1895 when, along with two others, he founded the National Trust. The Trust is the largest landowner in the Lake District National Park, protecting over a quarter of the area including nearly all the high central fells, many of the lakes, more than eighty working farms and over 250 houses and cottages.

In the 1974 reform of county boundaries the government – recognising the unity of the 'Lake counties' – designated that all of Cumberland and Westmorland and parts of Lancashire and the West Riding of Yorkshire should become the new county of Cumbria.

If Wordsworth was concerned about the increasing number of tourists attracted to the English Lakes in the early nineteenth century, he would have been horrified by the enormous volume of people visiting the area today: 12 million a year! Day-trippers, holidaymakers, fell walkers, rock climbers, naturalists, geologists, botanists, boating enthusiasts, campers, artists, writers and photographers – the list is endless. And since the early journals and guide-books of Gray (1775), West (1778), Gilpin (1786) and Wordsworth (1810), over 50,000 books have been written about the Lakes.

The popularity and uniqueness of the English Lakes lies not only in the landscape, with its wealth of historical and literary associations, but also in the character, life and traditions of its people: the shepherds and farmers, the quarrymen and miners, the foresters and charcoal burners, the weavers and bobbin makers, the dry-stone-wallers and all the other rural craftsmen.

Out of the working life of the dalesmen – out of doors day after day on the fells – has grown a number of distinctly Cumbrian sports for which great strength and stamina is essential: fell running, wrestling, hound trailing and fox hunting (not on horseback but on foot) – all rarely seen outside the region. Each year there are major sporting events throughout Lakeland, the largest at Grasmere. 'The Grasmere Sports are to the dalesmen of Westmorland and Cumberland what the gathering for the Highland games is to men across the border,' wrote Canon Rawnsley after he had left Keswick to spend his retirement in the vale of Grasmere. 'Everyone goes to "Girsmer" on Sports' Day.'

Despite its comparatively small area and the fears of people like Rawnsley and Wordsworth that industry and tourism would destroy the remarkable beauty of the landscape, the Lakes have not been ruined. They have survived, a magnificent jewel in England's crown, there for all who have 'an eye to perceive and a heart to enjoy'.

BIRKS RAPIDS,
DUDDON VALLEY

From the river's source to its estuary the twelve-mile-long Duddon Valley is full of variety and beauty. Beginning on desolate fells, near Wrynose Pass, the valley broadens below Cockley Beck and is soon covered by a dense forest of conifers. In the years since 1936 the eastern slopes of Harter Fell (which drop steeply into the valley) have been planted with trees to a height of 1,500 feet. Afforestation began in the area around Birks Farm and has now spread both northwards and southwards, following the craggy western side of the Duddon for over two miles. Beneath the Dunnerdale Forest, and below Birks Rapids and Birks Bridge, the river narrows and is squeezed between a deep cleft in the rock. Further down the valley the water, clear and blue-green in colour, races through the steep and thickly wooded Wallowbarrow Gorge to Seathwaite.

Ambleside & the Central Lakes

GRASMERE from Red Bank Woods

Clouds, lingering yet, extend in solid bars
Through the grey west; and lo! these waters, steeled
By breezeless air to smoothest polish, yield
A vivid repetition of the stars.

Wordsworth composed these lines by the side of Grasmere lake in 1807, thankfully proclaiming that

. . .if unholy deeds
Ravage the world, tranquility is here!

The lake is small, a mile long, half a mile wide and 75 feet at its deepest. The white building on the shore is the Prince of Wales Hotel, where Wordsworth launched and landed his boat when he lived at Dove Cottage, Town End. The lake contains trout, pike and perch and the poet often went out in his boat to fish.

In her journal on 15 April 1802 Dorothy Wordsworth wrote:

> When we were in the wood beyond Gowbarrow Park, we saw a few daffodils close to the water-side. . . . But as we went along there were more and yet more; and at last, under the boughs of the trees, we saw that there was a long belt of them running along the shore, about the breadth of a country turnpike road. I never saw daffodils so beautiful.

It was this scene, on the northern banks of Ullswater in the eastern Lakes, which inspired William Wordsworth to write his famous poem about daffodils – 'I wandered lonely as a cloud . . .' – one of the most memorized poems in the English language.

William Wordsworth and his sister Dorothy were born at Cockermouth and spent most of their long lives in the Lakes, moving to Grasmere in 1799 and later to Rydal. They are both buried, with other members of the Wordsworth family, in a spot chosen by the poet himself – a tree shaded corner of St Oswald's churchyard, Grasmere, beside the trout-filled waters of the River Rothay. This spot has now become one of the great literary shrines, attracting visitors from all over the world into the heart and centre of Lakeland. The Wordsworths, their lives and their works, stand supreme in the literary landscape of Lakeland. Yet there are many other writers, past and present, whose names will always be associated with the region.

Even when he was alive, Wordsworth acted as a magnet, attracting some of the great literary figures of his time to the Lakes to visit or to live. Samuel Taylor Coleridge, Robert Southey and Thomas De Quincey are sometimes, with Wordsworth, referred to as the Lake Poets. Sir Walter Scott, John Keats, Charles Lamb, Percy Bysshe Shelley spent time there, as did Lord Alfred Tennyson, who composed much of his poem *Morte d'Arthur* on the shores of Bassenthwaite Lake. Nathaniel Hawthorne, Charles Dickens and Charlotte Brontë are among others of note.

Dr Thomas Arnold, the famous headmaster of Rugby School, built Fox How as a holiday home in 1834 in the delightful Rothay Valley between Rydal and Ambleside.

Charlotte Brontë described it as 'a nest, half buried in flowers'. The Arnolds were friends of the Wordsworths, who only lived a short distance away.

John Ruskin – whom Tolstoy called 'one of the most remarkable of men, not only of England and our time, but of all countries and all times' – is buried in Coniston churchyard. From 1872 until his death in 1900 he lived at Brantwood in the southern Lakes, overlooking Coniston Water. Not only was he a writer, he was also an art critic, an artist, a champion of the Pre-Raphaelites, a social reformer and a pioneer of the conservation movement. Canon Rawnsley and Octavia Hill (two of the three founders of the National Trust) were his students and admirers.

More recently, Coniston Water was the setting for Arthur Ransome's *Swallows and Amazons*, published in 1930. The Duddon Valley, the inspiration for no less than thirty-four of Wordsworth's sonnets, was also the setting for Richard Adams's best-selling novel *Plague Dogs*, published in 1977.

Although the beauty and variety of Lakeland's scenery has inspired many literary figures, others have been fascinated by the life and traditions of the people who live and work on the fells and in the dales: the shepherds, quarry men, miners and foresters. Sir Hugh Walpole, in his *Herries Chronicle* (published between 1930 and 1933), records the scenes from the life of a Cumberland family 'during two hundred years of change and fortune'. The novels, consisting of *Rogue Herries*, *Judith Paris*, *The Fortress* and *Vanessa*, were set in the western and northern Lakes and mainly around Keswick.

Many modern writers and poets have been born or have chosen to live and work in and around Lakeland: Norman Nicholson (who died in 1987), Melvyn Bragg, Hunter Davies and John Wyatt, to name but a few.

The most-visited residence of a Lakeland writer – more popular even than Wordsworth's Dove Cottage in Grasmere – is Hill Top, at Near Sawrey, in the southern Lakes. This was the home of Beatrix Potter (or Mrs Heelis, as she preferred to be called) whose tales of Peter Rabbit, Mrs Tiggy-Winkle and Jemima Puddleduck have delighted children and parents alike since her first illustrated book was published in 1901.

The richest concentration of famous literary properties is around Ambleside, however, in the central Lakes. It was to this area of outstanding beauty, that William and Dorothy Wordsworth, Thomas De Quincey, Matthew Arnold, Harriet Martineau and Hartley Coleridge, among others, all came to live.

STOCK BECK,
AMBLESIDE

Stock Beck rises on the prominent whale-back mass of Red Screes (the 2,541-foot-high fell that towers above Kirkstone Pass) and tumbles south-westwards down the valley and over Stock Ghyll Force to Ambleside, below which it flows ino the River Rothay and eventually into Windermere. Stock Ghyll is derived from the old Norse words *stokkr*, meaning 'a tree stump', and *gil*, 'a narrow ravine'. It is possible, however, that 'stock' may also refer to one of several water-mills that were known to have existed in the valley, the earliest dating back to the early Middle Ages. Within a quarter-mile stretch of the Stock at Ambleside there was a corn-mill, a woollen-mill, a bobbin-mill and a bark-crushing-mill – all powered by the fast-flowing stream which after heavy rain can turn into a raging torrent, bringing stones and branches down from the fellsides and into the town.

DOVE COTTAGE, GRASMERE

In December 1799 Wordsworth and his sister Dorothy moved to a small cottage at Town End, Grasmere. They lived here for eight productive years: he produced many of his greatest works, and she not only wrote her *Grasmere Journal (1800–1803)* but also acted as his housekeeper, secretary and beloved companion. When William married in October 1802 he brought his new wife to the cottage to live with them. Although Dorothy was upset on the day of their wedding, she quickly came to terms with the arrangement, pleased that William had married her best friend and not someone who was a complete stranger. From then on, Wordsworth found that he had two women to look after him devotedly. Three of his children were born here.

During the period of the Wordsworths' residence the cottage did not have a name, nor did they give it one. Only later did it become known as Dove Cottage, because it had once been an inn called the Dove and Olive Branch.

DOVE COTTAGE, GRASMERE

When De Quincey, who later took over the tenancy of Dove Cottage, visited the Wordsworths on 4 November 1807, he wrote in his *Recollections of the Lakes and the Lake Poets*: 'A little semi-vestibule between two doors prefaced the entrance into what might be considered the principal room of the cottage. It was an oblong square, not above eight and a half feet high, sixteen feet long, and twelve broad; very prettily wainscotted from the floor to the ceiling with dark polished oak, slightly embellished with carving.' The kitchen (shown in the photograph) lies beyond the 'rustic hall', its small high, rose-framed window facing west to allow in the warm light of the afternoon. To the left of the cast-iron fireplace is a coal cellar and a small pantry.

The property is owned by the Wordsworth Trust, who have kept it much as it was during Wordsworth's time. Next door, in a converted barn, is the Wordsworth Museum, with a shop and restaurant.

ST OSWALD'S CHURCHYARD, GRASMERE

In June 1811 the Wordsworths moved from Allan Bank to the Old Rectory opposite the church of St Oswald, Grasmere. According to Sara Hutchinson, who was living with them, the house was 'in a deadly situation', sited on undrained land which made it cold, damp and unhealthy. In the two years that Wordsworth lived there he lost two of his five children, Catherine and Thomas, who were both buried in the churchyard near the spot which the poet himself chose for his final resting place. In order to improve the appearance of the churchyard he planted eight yew trees, and under the shadow of one, beside the River Rothay, is his grave. The inscription is simple: 'William Wordsworth 1850'. His wife Mary, who died nine years later, is buried with him. To the right of their gravestone lies their daughter, Dora, who married Edward Quillinan in 1841. Dorothy and Sara Hutchinson rest close by along with other members of the Wordsworth family.

ST OSWALD'S CHURCH, GRASMERE

The church at Grasmere is dedicated to Oswald, the seventh-century Christian ruler of Northumbria, who was killed near Hexham in a battle with Penda, king of Mercia, in 642 AD. The oldest part of the present building dates from the thirteenth century, but there has probably been a church on the site since Saxon times. Although the exterior is drab and somewhat featureless, hidden beneath a thick coat of roughcast, the interior is striking, with an unusual raftered roof dating back to 1562, which was described by Wordsworth in *The Excursion: Book V*. The floor of the church was earthen until 1881, and every year for hundreds of years there was a rush-bearing ceremony in which rushes and bracken were laid on the floor to make it warm and dry. This ceremony still survives today and is held on the Saturday nearest the fifth of August, St Oswald's Day, when the children who take part are rewarded with a piece of traditional gingerbread.

The rich and poor
the Lord is the maker of

RIVER ROTHAY,
WHITE MOSS COMMON

It is said that the char and trout of Windermere swim upstream together at the approach of the spawning season, until they reach the confluence of the Brathay and the Rothay. There they separate, the char going up the Brathay and the trout up the Rothay. Whether or not there is any truth in this curious arrangement, it is a known fact that the Rothay has been associated with trout for centuries. The name itself is derived from the old Norse for 'the river of the red one' or 'the trout river'. Rising near Dunmail Raise, south of Thirlmere, it flows south to Windermere, winding its way through Grasmere, Rydal Water and the green meadows, pastures and woods north of Ambleside. Between Grasmere and Rydal Water (where the photograph was taken) the National Trust have planted mixed hardwood trees and transformed land once strewn with waste from nearby quarries into a popular picnic area with pleasant walks alongside the swift-flowing river.

RYDAL WATER

The deep, steep-sided valley that contains the two lakes of Grasmere and Rydal Water was formed by the grinding action of boulder-strewn glacial ice; the debris left behind by the glaciers accounts for some of the islands. Rydal Water has two main islands, both wooded, and it was on the largest that Sir William Le Fleming, who died in 1736, attempted to build a pleasure house. According to Wordsworth, the project was abandoned, leaving an unfinished ruin, because Sir William learned: 'That from the shore a full-grown man might wade, And make himself a freeman of this spot. At any hour he chose.' The Le Flemings, an important landowning family, once owned Rydal Hall, situated above the village at the eastern end on the lake. It was Lady Diana Le Fleming who owned Rydal Mount during the early years of Wordsworth's tenancy and who also built the nearby church of St Mary, consecrated in 1825. Rydal Water means 'the lake in the valley where the rye is grown'.

RYDAL MOUNT, RYDAL

After living at Grasmere from 1799 to 1813 the Wordsworths moved to Rydal Mount, a large rented house on the wooded hillside above the church of St Mary, Rydal. By then the household had grown to include William, his wife Mary, his three surviving children John, Dora and William, his sister Dorothy and his sister-in-law Sara Hutchinson. The four adults were to reside at Rydal Mount for the rest of their lives, William himself dying there at eighty years of age on 23 April 1850. The house was originally a small farm cottage built in the mid-sixteenth century, but it was extended and improved in the mid-eighteenth century. The four and a half acres of informal terraced garden has changed little since it was designed by Wordsworth over 130 years ago. In front of the house, beyond the gravel forecourt, is an ancient mound or mount from which the house takes its name. It was once a beacon site and from it there is a distant view across Windermere to Belle Isle and Bowness beyond.

RYDAL MOUNT, RYDAL

In 1574 Rydal Mount was a small farm cottage with its entrance opening into what was then the living room, one of the oldest parts of the house. In the mid-eighteenth century, when further rooms were added, the original entrance in the east wall was sealed. Now the entrance faces south and leads into the hall. The old living room became a dining room and was used as such by Wordsworth. The portrait over the fireplace is of Sir Walter Scott, a man whose work Wordsworth greatly admired. To the left of the fireplace and built into the thick exterior wall is a little oak spice cupboard. It bears the date 1710 and the initials of Edward Knott, whose family owned the house for eighty years from 1700. The two candlesticks on the table were made from one of the yew trees that Wordsworth planted in Grasmere churchyard in 1819. The needlework on the seats of the chairs was worked by Dorothy, Mary and Sara Hutchinson. The house is now owned by the poet's great-great-granddaughter.

DORA'S FIELD, RYDAL

From the moment Wordsworth moved into Rydal Mount in 1813 he found cause to complain to the owners, the Le Flemings of Rydal Hall, about its poor state of repair. Relations between them at times became strained. In 1825, when it became known that they were thinking of letting the house to a relative, Wordsworth protested strongly; he definitely did not want to move and he did all he could to prevent it. He immediately purchased an adjoining field, next to the newly erected chapel and property of the Le Flemings, with the intention of building a new home upon it should he be evicted. In the end, however, they relented and the poet and his family were allowed to stay. The field, known as the Rashfield (because of the rushes that once grew in it), Wordsworth planted with daffodils and eventually gave to his favourite daughter, Dora. In 1935 his grandson, Gordon Wordsworth, gave it to the National Trust.

SCANDALE BECK, AMBLESIDE

From Hartsop, near Brothers Water, an ancient track climbs southwards over Scandale Pass (1,750 feet) and down into the valley of the Scandale Beck to Ambleside. The Beck rises near Scandale Tarn, fed by innumerable mountain streams from the surrounding fells of Red Screes, High Pike and Dove Crag. As with many rivers in Lakeland, its source is lost in the flat marshy depressions that are often found beneath the craggy heights. Within a short distance the trickling waters form a network of fast-flowing streams, tumbling over rocks and stones, plummeting through gullies and ravines, until they gather into a powerful river rushing to feed the lake and eventually the sea. The Scandale Beck flows under two old packhorse bridges – High Sweden Bridge and Low Sweden Bridge – before entering the River Rothay near Ambleside. Scandale and Sweden are both derived from Old Norse words, the former meaning 'the short dale' and the latter 'a clearing made by burning'.

BRIDGE HOUSE,
AMBLESIDE

The market town of Ambleside nestles in a green valley near the northern end of Windermere and in the heart and centre of Lakeland. The Romans built two forts at Galava, near the confluence of the rivers Brathay and Rothay, but the first recorded reference to Ambleside was in 1275 when it was known as *Amelsate*, from the Old Norse words meaning 'the pastures by the river sandbanks'. The town was granted its market charter in 1650. Although it contains many seventeenth-century buildings, its main expansion occurred in the nineteenth century. Bridge House, a small, quaint dollshouse-like dwelling, was built in the seventeenth century by the Braithwaites of Ambleside Hall, possibly as a summer house and also as a means of crossing over Stock Beck. A chair repairer and his wife lived there in the nineteenth century, reputedly bringing up their six children in its two tiny rooms. The house has an oven, a chimney and an outside staircase leading to the first floor, and is now used as a National Trust Information Centre.

RYDAL CAVE,
LOUGHRIGG FELL

Loughrigg Fell is a sprawling mass of rough country rising to a height of 1,101 feet between the Brathay and Rothay river valleys. Loughrigg means the 'ridge above the lake' although, in fact, it directly overlooks two lakes, Grasmere and Rydal Water, the popular path along Loughrigg Terrace connecting them both. On the northern side of the fell, above Rydal Water, are the abandoned workings of Loughrigg quarries. Here there is a massive cavern which, according to Wainwright, could shelter 'the whole population of Ambleside (although admittedly many people would be standing in water)'. It looks over the lake to Nab Scar and was originally quarried for its blue slate, examples of which can be found on the man-made plateau of spoil near the entrance. The history of quarrying as an organised industry in Lakeland can be traced back to the mid-seventeenth century when the workings at Honister were in production. Although most small workings have been abandoned, slate is still being quarried in a number of places for use as a building material.

LOUGHRIGG TARN

In 1811 Wordsworth wrote an *Epistle to Sir George Howland Beaumont, Bart.* Beaumont was a wealthy landowner, amateur painter and one of the founders of the National Gallery; he was also the poet's friend and patron, and it was probably because Loughrigg Tarn was part of the Beaumont estate that Wordsworth mentioned it in the poem, calling it 'Diana's Looking-glass' after a lake near Rome. Thirty years later he explained: 'Loughrigg Tarn, alluded to in the foregoing Epistle, resembles, though much smaller in compass, the Lake Nemi, or *Speculum Dianae* as it is often called, not only in its clear waters and circular form, and the beauty immediately surrounding it, but also as being overlooked by the eminence of Langdale Pikes as Lake Nemi is by that of Monte Calvo.' Loughrigg Tarn is situated on the south-west side of Loughrigg Fell and Wordsworth's description in his guide to the Lakes is still appropriate: 'It has a margin of green firm meadows, of rocks, and rocky woods, a few reeds here, a little company of waterlilies there.'

STOCK GHYLL FORCE, AMBLESIDE

Stock Ghyll Force, about half a mile north-east of Ambleside, is reached by a steep road that runs behind the Salutation Hotel. A few hundred yards up the road, an entrance on the left leads into an attractive wooded park with paths on both sides of the ravine. The fall itself is pretty rather than spectacular, the water passing under a footbridge where it is split by projecting rocks to cascade some 90 feet into a rock-pool. A few years before his death in 1821 John Keats visited the waterfall and wrote in his *Letters*: 'What astonishes me more than anything is the tone, the colouring, the slate, the stone, the moss, the rock-weed; or, if I may so say, the intellect, the countenance of such places. The space, the magnitude of mountains and waterfalls are well imagined before one sees them; but this countenance or intellectual tone must surpass every imagination and defy remembrance. I shall learn poetry here and shall henceforth write more than ever. . . .'

RIVER BRATHAY, SKELWITH

From beneath the summits of the craggy fells towering above Great and Little Langdale numerous becks and gills tumble down into the valleys to create two rushing streams, the Great Langdale Beck and the River Brathay, which combine in Elterwater. The source of the Brathay is on Pike o' Blisco, near Wrynose Pass. It then flows eastwards through Little Langdale Tarn and Elterwater to the Roman fort of Galava, where it merges with the Rothay before entering Windermere. Brathay is an Old Norse word for 'the broad river' and probably refers to its fairly wide lower reaches. Below Elterwater, at Skelwith Force near Skelwith Bridge, the river is squeezed between a narrow cleft of rock, and after heavy rain – despite having only a fifteen- or twenty-foot drop – the power of the fall is tremendous, carrying what is possibly the greatest volume of water in Lakeland. At such times the valley between Skelwith and Clappersgate often floods (as has happened in the photograph) and the river becomes one vast lake.

ELTERWATER from Rob Rash Wood

In the late eighteenth and nineteenth centuries the increasing demand from the slate quarries and copper mines of the Coniston and Keswick areas for gunpowder led to the development of local gunpowder works. In 1824 mills were opened at a site north of the village of Elterwater with power from the Great Langdale Beck and charcoal, one of the main components, from the surrounding woodland. The additional ingredients of saltpetre and sulphur were brought by boat either up Coniston water to Waterhead or up Windermere to the River Brathay, from where they were unloaded and transported overland. The mills closed in 1928–9. The Great Langdale Beck and the River Brathay meet in the irregular reed-fringed lake of Elterwater which, like many of the lakes, is gradually getting smaller because of the accumulation of silt and other river-borne material. The infilling process has been going on steadily since the last glaciation, and eventually Elterwater will disappear.

ELTERWATER
from the north-east shore

Elterwater, only half a mile long, is the smallest of the sixteen lakes and lies at the junction of the Great and Little Langdale valleys. It is a shallow, irregularly shaped lake which receives the waters of both valleys before they emerge as the River Brathay to pour down the dramatic Skelwith waterfalls and head in an easterly direction to Windermere. The banks of the lake are reeded and are a favourite haunt of a large variety of waterfowl including herons, coots, moorhens, mallards, tufted ducks, grebes, mergansers and mute swans. Elterwater is an Old Norse name meaning 'lake of swans' and even today it is often visited in winter by the whooper swan. The village of Elterwater is situated to the north-west of the lake, just before the valley opens out into Great Langdale. Many of the houses and cottages are built of local slate which has an attractive green colour. The snow-covered peaks in the centre of the photograph are the distinctive Langdale Pikes.

BLEA TARN, LANGDALE

To the west of Elterwater is Lingmoor Fell (1,530 feet) which separates Great Langdale from Little Langdale. The two valleys are linked by a narrow, winding road that follows the course of Bleamoss Beck, climbing the side of the fell, to pass Bleatarn House, the home of Wordsworth's 'Solitary' (*The Excursion: Book II*). In the poem he describes the house as 'one bare dwelling; one abode, no more' and the nearby tarn as 'a liquid pool that glittered in the sun'. Having approached the valley from the top of Lingmoor Fell, he goes on to write

> . . . full many a spot
> Of hidden beauty have I
> chanced to espy
> Among the mountains; never
> one like this;
> So lonesome, and so
> perfectly secure.

Alas, no more! Blea Tarn, whose name means the dark or deep blue tarn, is now a popular spot for families, who come in droves to picnic on the water's edge. The Langdale Pikes are on the right of the photograph.

LITTLE LANGDALE
from Castle Howe

The narrow, winding road that links the two Langdales heads north from near Fell Foot Farm, Little Langdale, then climbs the side of Lingmoor Fell and passes Blea Tarn to descend steeply into Great Langdale, where the snow-covered Langdale Pikes rise abruptly from the Mickleden valley. The small northerly urn-shaped arm of the Little Langdale valley, through which the road runs, provided the setting for Wordsworth's 'Solitary'. At Castle Howe, close to Fell Foot Farm, there is a strange, terraced mound which is thought to be a 'thing-mount', a meeting-place used by the Norse settlers. Today the area is often used for the popular Lakeland betting sport of hound trailing in which specially trained dogs follow a scent, laid earlier, around a circular course that takes them down into the marshy valley, over fences and walls, and up onto the rocky fellsides.

LITTLE LANGDALE
from Wrynose

The head-waters of the River Brathay rise on the rugged slopes of Pike o' Blisco near Wrynose Pass – where the old Three Shire Stone marks the meeting of the three old counties of Cumberland, Westmorland and Lancashire – and flow east down the valley to feed Little Langdale Tarn. To the south of this small shallow tarn the curving slopes of Wetherlam rise steeply to reach 2,502 feet at the summit. On the opposite side of the valley the old Roman road from Wrynose Pass winds down the south-eastern side of Pike o' Blisco for about two miles to Fell Foot Farm. The farm was once an inn where packmen and their animals rested before making the arduous ascent over the pass into the Duddon Valley. Like the mist that rises from the valley bottom the region is shrouded in tales of mystery, particularly smuggling and the exploits of the legendary Lanty Slee, who operated a number of illicit distilleries in hideouts high up in the fells around Wrynose.

STICKLE TARN,
PAVEY ARK

Pavey Ark, 2,228 feet above sea-level, is a precipitous cliff of grey rock which plunges vertically to the waters of Stickle Tarn, over 700 feet below. Although geographically it forms the eastern edge of Thunacar Knott (2,351 feet), Wainwright considers Pavey Ark to be 'one of the greatest precipices in the district'. Pavey Ark is the easternmost of the five summits forming the arc of Langdale Pikes, all overlooking Great Langdale. The others are Harrison Stickle, Thorn Crag, Loft Crag and Pike o' Stickle. There are a number of ascents from Stickle Tarn to the summit cairn on Pavey Ark, but the most impressive is the route up the diagonal gash of Jack's Rake, which is more of a rock climb than a walk. The stream which issues from Stickle Tarn forms the Mill Gill (Stickle Ghyll) and drops down the fellside in a series of cataracts to enter the Great Langdale Beck in Great Langdale. At the south-eastern end of the tarn is a dam, built for the former gunpowder factory at Elterwater.

LOFT CRAG AND GREAT LANGDALE
from Pike o' Stickle

Loft Crag is one of the five summits of the Langdale Pikes, standing between Pike o' Stickle and Thorn Crag. Overlooking Great Langdale it is the third highest of the group at 2,270 feet, with magnificent views down the valley and across Lingmoor Fell towards Windermere. Gimmer Crag, the spectacular south-east face of Loft Crag, soars steeply above Mickleden and is extremely popular for rock climbing. From the valley floor a steep and impressive wall of rock sweeps upwards without interruption nearly 2,000 feet to the tapering thimble-like peak of Pike o' Stickle (2,323 feet). Hidden among the scree of Pike o' Stickle's eastern face is a small man-made cave, probably used over 4,000 years ago in the manufacture of stone axes. (In the photograph the peak in the foreground is Loft Crag. The large lake to the left of the summit is Windermere and below it is Elterwater. Gimmer Crag lies to the right of Loft Crag and in the valley beyond is Blea Tarn, Langdale).

KESWICK & THE NORTHERN LAKES

CASTLERIGG STONE CIRCLE, KESWICK

Wordsworth was fascinated by the druids and believed, like many people at that time, that the mysterious circles, henges and monoliths found scattered throughout the British Isles were built by them in about the first century BC. Thus it was that Castlerigg Stone Circle was popularly known as the Druids' Circle, even though it was considerably older, probably with origins in the Bronze Age (*c.* 1500 BC). Surrounded by a ring of high fells, this megalithic monument stands on a magnificent site, two miles east of Keswick. The circle – more oval than round – is about a 100 feet in diameter and comprises thirty-eight rough-hewn stones with a further ten forming a rectangle on the east side. The largest stone is over 7 feet tall and weighs several tons, but most are unimpressive. It was purchased in 1913 by Canon Rawnsley and others, on behalf of the National Trust.

In 1947 a stone axe-making factory was discovered on the tumbling screes of Pike o' Stickle, high above the valley floor in Great Langdale. Dating from around 2,500 BC – when the area was covered with a dense forest – it was worked by the Neolithic or New Stone Age people, who had by then penetrated the heart of Lakeland and established similar factories on Glaramara, Great End, Scafell and Scafell Pike. The axes were made from an extremely hard rock, formed by a finely grained volcanic ash, which chips like flint to produce a sharp cutting edge. Roughed out on the site and taken to the coast for polishing and sharpening, these Cumbrian stone axes have been found in Ireland, the Isle of Man, Scotland, Wales and as far south as Dorset in England.

Axe-making was Lakeland's first major industry and, with access to what proved to be a very effective tool, the Neolithic settlers could then begin to clear the trees and cultivate the land. On the remote, windswept fells around Devoke Water in the western Lakes – well away from the marshy and unworkable valley bottoms – these early farmers (who grew cereal crops and reared animals) have left behind literally hundreds of prehistoric remains, including burial mounds, cairns and stone circles.

The rocks and minerals of the region have been exploited by man since prehistoric times. The great stone circles found at Little Salkeld (Long Meg and her daughters), at Castlerigg, near Keswick, and at Swinside, near Broughton-in-Furness, were probably built by Bronze Age settlers, who arrived in Cumbria from Spain and France around 1,500 BC. These primitive farmers had developed sufficient metallurgical skills to make bronze – a brown alloy consisting mainly of copper and tin – and were, therefore, able to produce more efficient tools and weapons.

Although it is generally maintained that the Iron Age began in approximately 500 BC, it is thought that the people of Lakeland remained in the Bronze Age until the arrival of the Romans, who invaded Britain in 43 AD. By the end of the century they had reached Cumbria and had established control of the lowlands around the fringes of the Lakes.

Not long after their arrival in Lakeland the Roman military engineers – using the local quarried stone as building material – constructed a military road from the port of

Ravenglass on the western coast to Ambleside in the central Lakes, with a fort at either end and one in the middle at Hardknott.

Lakeland contains a variety of rocks, from the soft Skiddaw Slates to the hard Borrowdale Volcanics, but only some are suitable for use as building materials – slate, sandstone, limestone and granite, for example. The Romans, however, not only made use of the rocks for construction purposes but also exploited them for their mineral wealth. Some of the old mine workings scarring the open fellsides, particularly around the Coniston area, are thought to date from Roman times.

However, it was not until the middle of the sixteenth century – when the Company of Mines Royal imported a work-force of highly skilled German miners into the region – that large-scale exploitation of Lakeland's mineral wealth began. The company (established in 1561) opened their first mines in the Newlands Valley, to the west of Derwentwater, and the copper ore was smelted at Keswick, which quickly developed into a prosperous little mining town. Further mines were opened in the Coniston area, particularly in the Coppermines Valley, and the ore was laboriously transported by pack-horses over the fells to Keswick. A third mining area, on the Caldbeck Fells at the 'back o' Skidda', produced not only copper, but other minerals, including zinc, barytes, manganese and lead.

The world's first pencil factory was opened in Keswick in 1566, using 'wad' (black lead or graphite) from the mines at Seathwaite in Borrowdale. The factory still exists and continues to produce pencils, although the lead is now imported.

In almost every valley in Lakeland there was some form of mining activity – providing work not only for the miners, but also for the craftsmen whose skills were required to service the industry: haematite (a red iron ore) was mined in the western Lakes, particularly at Eskdale; wolfram – an ore of tungsten – was worked in the Caldew Valley, north of Blencathra; and lead was mined in the valley of the Glenridding Beck, on the eastern side of the Helvellyn range.

During the eighteenth century mining began to decline and, although a number of mines continued to be worked intermittently right up until the 1960s, the majority were abandoned. The quarrying industry in Lakeland – dating back to the stone axe-making factories of Neolithic man – has also declined and only a few survive, mainly producing ornamental and architectural slate.

JAWS OF BORROWDALE
from Derwentwater

'The pride of Lake Keswick is the head, where the mountains of Borrowdale bound the prospect, in a wilder and grander manner than words can describe.' Of course the Lake Keswick described by Southey is Derwentwater. The Jaws of Borrowdale are situated at the southern end of the lake where the River Derwent passes through a thickly wooded gorge before entering Derwentwater.

Derwentwater, known as the 'Queen of the Lakes', is four miles long, one and a quarter miles wide and 72 feet deep. It has four main islands: Derwent Island, on which there once lived German miners, and later an eccentric called Pocklington; Lord's Island, on which used to be the house of the Earl of Derwentwater; St Herbert's Island, named after a disciple of St Cuthbert; and Rampsholme Island. There is another 'island': a floating island which appears every three years or so and consists of a mass of weeds and rotting vegetation brought to the surface by marsh gases.

LODORE FALLS,
BORROWDALE

'Tell the people how the water comes down Lodore?', Southey wrote to his brother in 1809. 'Why it comes thundering and floundering, and thumping and plumping and bumping and jumping and hissing and whizzing and dripping and skipping and grumbling and rumbling and tumbling and falling and brawling, dashing and clashing and splashing, and purring and roaring and whirling and curling, and leaping and creeping, and sounding and bounding, and clattering and chattering, with a dreadful uproar – and that way the water comes down at Lodore.' Thirteen years later he converted his prose into a more famous poem about the falls, but it is only after a heavy storm, high up on the Watendlath Fells and High Seat, that the waterfall anything like approaches his description. Most of the time it is split by boulders into a multitude of small cascades and, in dry weather, it shrivels to little more than a trickle. Lodore Falls is situated behind the Lodore Hotel at the southern end of Derwentwater.

KESWICK
from Latrigg

Keswick, the capital of northern Lakeland, is delightfully situated: it nestles in a green vale, on the banks of the River Greta, and is set gem-like between Derwentwater and the impressive bulks of Skiddaw and Blencathra. Originally a small wool-market town, Keswick became the prosperous centre of northern Lakeland's mining industry in the sixteenth century. By the middle of the eighteenth century the town was described as 'greatly decayed and much inferior to what it was formerly'. However, when tourists began to discover the Lakes in the early nineteenth century, Keswick underwent a revival. In 1800 Samuel Taylor Coleridge took up residence at Greta Hall (now part of Keswick School) and, later, Robert Southey moved in. Before renting Dove Cottage, Wordsworth and Dorothy lived for a while at Old Windebrowe, overlooking the town. The stone and slate houses, lining the narrow streets of Keswick, are mostly Victorian. The Moot Hall, standing in the market square, was rebuilt in 1813 and is now an Information Centre.

ASHNESS BRIDGE, BORROWDALE

Ashness Gill rises on the heather-clad slopes of High Seat (1,995 feet) and cascades down the fellside to pass under Ashness Bridge, before entering Derwentwater near Barrow Bay. The stone bridge, with its single small arch, is wider than most, and was probably built at the beginning of the eighteenth century. It is situated on the narrow, winding Watendlath road (which begins to climb steeply from the Borrowdale road two miles south of Keswick). It is the most famous bridge in Lakeland and was originally used by pack-horses on the old route from Keswick to Watendlath. Looking north-westwards the view includes Derwentwater and distant Bassenthwaite Lake. Keswick nestles at the foot of mighty Skiddaw which, at 3,053 feet, is the fourth highest peak in Lakeland. Ashness means 'the headland where the ash trees grow' and they can still be found – along with oak, holly, sycamore, beech and fir – in nearby Ashness Woods, owned by the National Trust.

GRANGE, BORROWDALE

In 1769 Thomas Gray ventured into Borrowdale, terrified that the 'dreadful bulk' of rock overhanging the boulder-strewn road might tumble down on him. As the steep, wooded fellsides closed in around him, narrowing towards the Jaws of Borrowdale, he declined to go any further and stopped at the tiny hamlet of Grange, convinced that 'all farther access is here barred to prying mortals'. Before the Dissolution of the Monasteries Grange was owned by the monks of Furness Abbey; indeed its name derives from the fact that it was once the site of their grange, or granary. The hamlet, consisting of a small church and a cluster of stone cottages, is famous for its double-arched pack-horse bridge which was built in 1675 and spans the River Derwent. The western end is constructed on *roche moutonnée*, rock that has been worn smooth and deeply scratched by the pressure of ice grinding over it during the Ice Age.

GRANGE FELL, BORROWDALE

Almost three quarters of a mile south of the village of Grange on the wooded slopes of Grange Fell below King's How stands the Bowder Stone. This enormous cube-shaped boulder, estimated to weigh 2,000 tons, is approximately 36 feet high and 60 feet long, with wooden steps on one side to allow visitors access to the top. The stone was popularly thought to have fallen from the crags above, but it is more likely that it was deposited – poised delicately on its edge – by melting glacial ice. If the geologist can find much that is fascinating in Borrowdale, so can the naturalist, for the area is noted for its rich variety of rare plants, birds and insects. The woods surrounding the stone consist mainly of the hardy birch, a tree that grows well on the poor soils of the fellsides. In other parts of the valley the woodland is mixed with oak, beech and alder predominating. Johnny Wood, between Seatoller and Rosthwaite, is protected by the National Trust as a Site of Special Scientific Interest.

WATENDLATH, BORROWDALE

Watendlath is a small, isolated moorland hamlet lying in a hidden valley high above and to the east of Borrowdale: a winding road that follows Watendlath Beck up over the famous Ashness Bridge and past some magnificent views of Derwentwater ends at a cluster of partly whitewashed cottages and farm buildings constructed mainly of slate (a major building material used in the region since the late seventeenth century). Watendlath was the remote setting for Hugh Walpole's *Judith Paris* (1931), the second of four novels that form the *Herries Chronicle*. The entire hamlet is protected by the National Trust which also owns Watendlath Tarn, Watendlath Bridge and all the surrounding land. It was not until 1978 that it received a mains electricity supply, the last place in Lakeland to be connected. A footpath to the east, crossing exceedingly wet and marshy ground, leads up and over the dark heathery mound of High Tove (1,665 feet) and down to Armboth on Thirlmere.

RIVER DERWENT,
BORROWDALE

Although numerous streams run down into the Derwent from the soaring heights above Borrowdale, the river's source is generally regarded as being near Sprinkling Tarn below Great End (2,984 feet), the domed summit that forms the north-eastern end of a ridge that climbs a further 226 feet to the top of Scafell Pike. Beginning as a mountain stream, the Derwent becomes a river near Rosthwaite, in the Borrowdale valley, where it is joined by the substantial Stonethwaite Beck. As the river passes from this broad and lush valley it is suddenly constricted into a narrow, steep-walled gorge known as the Jaws of Borrowdale. It emerges into a wide boulder-strewn valley where it flows north, entering Derwentwater and Bassenthwaite Lake, before turning west past Cockermouth to empty into the Irish Sea at Workington. The name of the River Derwent has Celtic origins and means the 'river which abounds in oak trees'.

STOCKLEY BRIDGE,
BORROWDALE

One of the popular routes to Scafell Pike begins at Seathwaite, the tiny hamlet that has the reputation of being the wettest place in England; it then follows a pack-horse track up to the head of the valley at Stockley Bridge, about 600 feet above sea-level. Here the waters of Grains Gill, the infant River Derwent, tumble into emerald-clear pools before making the rock-strewn descent into the lush and beautiful Borrowdale valley. In extremely wet weather the mountain stream quickly becomes a raging torrent, picking up stones and boulders on its downward course. At such times – as happened in the storm floods of 1966 – the bridge is liable to get damaged. Carefully restored and preserved by the National Trust, this is a fine example of a Cumbrian pack-horse bridge. It is situated on what was probably one of the busiest of all Lakeland pack-routes, linking Borrowdale not only with Wasdale, via the 1,600-foot high Sty Head Pass, but also with Great Langdale, via Esk Hause.

SWALEDALE SHEEP, HONISTER HAUSE

The Swaledale, with its distinctive grey muzzle and black face, was introduced into Lakeland from the northern Pennines and has tended to displace the traditional Herdwick, which is now mainly found on the central and western fells. It is a finer-bodied sheep than the Herdwick, with a long, coarse outer coat and a dense undercoat that can withstand the coldest winds. Both the rams and the ewes have long, curved horns, which are used locally for making ornately carved shepherd's crooks and walking sticks. Like the Herdwick, the Swaledale is noted for its strong homing instinct, which tends to keep it in the particular part, or *heaf*, of the open fell where it was raised by its mother. It is for this reason that when a farm is let to a new tenant it traditionally includes a flock of its fell sheep. Swaledale ewes, more likely to produce lambs than Herdwicks, are widely used for cross-breeding.

ROSTHWAITE AND STONETHWAITE, BORROWDALE

South of the Jaws of Borrowdale the Borrowdale valley opens out into a broad patchwork of green meadows and lush pastures with scattered farmsteads and hamlets nestling below the steep, wooded slopes and soaring crags of some of the most impressive fells in Lakeland. Rosthwaite is the largest of the four hamlets in the upper Borrowdale valley, lying on a rocky shelf above the flood plain of the River Derwent and below Brund Fell, the highest summit of the 1,363-foot-high Grange Fell. It consists of a cluster of farms and cottages with a post office and shop. In 1812 Wordsworth, on his way to visit Southey at Keswick, had to spend the night at one of its inns sharing a bed with a Scottish peddler, an inconvenience that he didn't seem to mind. Stonethwaite lies about three quarters of a mile south-east of Rosthwaite, and between them is the tiny whitewashed church of Borrowdale. Beyond, the valley snakes its way southwestwards to Seatoller.

NEWLANDS CHURCH, NEWLANDS VALLEY

On the western shore of Derwentwater a range of fells – rising in height from Cat Bells (1,481 feet) to High Spy (2,143 feet) – effectively separates the lake from the lush and fertile pastures of Newlands Valley. Newlands refers to the 'new lands' which were first cultivated in the fourteenth century after Uzzicar Tarn was drained. It was here, in the vicinity of Little Town, at 'the back of the hill called Cat Bells', that Beatrix Potter set *The Tale of Mrs Tiggy-Winkle*.

At Little Town the Keskadale Beck and the Scope Beck converge on Newlands Beck to flow north, as one stream, down the valley past the tiny hamlet of Stair. A short distance up the Keskadale Beck above Little Town is the small whitewashed church of Newlands, rebuilt in 1843 and restored in 1885. The small building adjoining the church is Newlands School, built by the parishioners in 1877, but closed in 1967. The church itself is the starting-point for many fine walks up the surrounding high fells.

NEWLANDS VALLEY

From Elizabethan times to the beginning of the nineteenth century the fells around Newlands echoed to the sound of workers mining for ore, particularly copper and lead. One of the oldest and richest mines in the area was the Goldscope Mine on the scarred east side of Scope End, above Newlands Beck. The tunnel workings penetrate deep into the fellside at different levels and were abandoned not because the minerals – which also included gold and silver – were exhausted, but because the depths of the shafts made it too costly to mine. Once an important industrial centre, the vale below the twin fells of Hindscarth (on the left of the photograph) and Robinson (on the right) is now lush and peaceful. The valley has three branches, each with its own beck. The route alongside the Keskadale Beck leads to Buttermere and Crummock Water, via the high pass of Newlands Hause.

SKIDDAW RANGE
from Bassenthwaite Lake

The eastern side of Bassenthwaite Lake is dominated by the prominent and isolated bulk of the Skiddaw range. Although it appears to be of no great height, Skiddaw is the fourth highest peak in Lakeland at 3,053 feet above sea-level; and it is only 110 feet lower than the highest, Scafell Pike. On Skiddaw's western side, overlooking the lake, is Dodd, described by Wainwright as 'a whelp of Skiddaw crouched at the feet of its parent'. However, in marked contrast to its bare 'old man', Dodd has been thickly clothed with trees, including the Sitka spruce, Douglas fir and Scots pine. Bassenthwaite village nestles in a valley over a mile from the lake, at the foot of Skiddaw's north-western slopes, with many of its houses grouped around the green. The church of St John, built in 1878, stands half a mile south of the village on the busy main road from Keswick to Carlisle. Bassenthwaite Lake has been owned by the Lake District Special Planning Board since 1979.

ST BEGA'S CHURCH,
BASSENTHWAITE

In the fourteenth century an unidentified monk wrote of Bega, the daughter of an Irish chieftain who lived in the seventh century, noting that 'the history of the early life and acts of St Bega is for the most part lost.' Apparently she decided as a child not to marry and vowed to dedicate her life to God. But she grew into a beautiful woman and her father, wishing to establish good relations with the Norsemen, arranged for her to marry 'the son of the King of Norway, and his heir'. On the eve of the wedding God helped her to escape: she fled across the sea to Cumberland, landing at St Bees Head. She founded a nunnery and dedicated herself to caring for the sick and poor of the region. Legend attributes many remarkable miracles to St Bega and the tiny church on the eastern shore of Bassenthwaite Lake beneath Skiddaw is dedicated to her. The oldest parts of the church, like the plain, unmoulded chancel arch, possibly date from the tenth or eleventh century, but it was drastically restored in 1874.

MIREHOUSE, BASSENTHWAITE

Three and a half miles north-west of Keswick, on the eastern shores of Bassenthwaite Lake and below the forested slopes of Skiddaw, stands Mirehouse, the home of the Speddings since 1802. James Spedding (1808–1881), who devoted most of his working life to the study of Francis Bacon, was a friend of many writers and poets, including three Poets Laureate: Wordsworth, Southey and Tennyson. They all came to visit him at Mirehouse and it is thought that it was here, on the shores of the lake, that Tennyson composed much of his poem *Morte d'Arthur* (published in 1842). The house is a typical English manor house dating from the seventeenth century, with nineteenth-century additions. It contains many rooms of interest, including the Smoking Room used by James Spedding and his visitors. There are also numerous portraits and manuscripts of Bacon, Tennyson and other literary figures. Modern attractions include an aventure playground, lakeside and forest walks and a tea room.

OVER WATER, ULDALE

Over Water, less than a quarter of a mile long, is situated amid trees and pastureland on the northernmost fringes of Lakeland, two miles north-east of the village of Bassenthwaite, and is just visible in the middle distance of the photograph. To the north is a stretch of wild and barren moorland and to the south is the distinctive peak of Skiddaw (in the centre of the photograph). Over Water and Little Tarn, near Orthwaite, which is even smaller, feed into the Chapelhouse Reservoir before joining the River Ellen which flows northwards and then westwards to enter the Irish Sea at Maryport. The grass-covered Uldale Fells rise smoothly and gently from the valley of the tarn to the summits of Great and Little Sca Fell.

Over is derived from an Old Norse word which was both a personal name and the name for a black grouse. The meaning of Over Water, therefore, is either 'Orri's tarn' or 'the tarn where the black grouse are found'.

ST KENTIGERN'S CHURCH, CALDBECK

Caldbeck, a small village of attractive stone-built houses, lies on the northern boundary of the National Park. It is famous for its association with John Peel, a tall, rough-spoken farmer and legendary huntsman, who was born here in 1776. When he was twenty-one he eloped with Mary White, a girl of only eighteen, and they were married at Gretna Green. In order to please their parents, who by then were resigned to the situation, they were remarried in Caldbeck church in December 1797. The Peels had thirteen children, seven sons and six daughters. Mary lived to be eighty-two years old, surviving her husband, who died at the age of seventy-eight and is buried in the churchyard.

The long, low, and ancient church of St Kentigern stands on the banks of a tributary of the River Caldew. It was built on the site of St Mungo's Well, the holy spring where St Kentigern (who was affectionately known as Mungo) used to baptise his converts in the sixth century.

ULDALE from near Green How

On the remote northern boundary of the National Park, Uldale is a small farming village with a wide green, fringed by stone buildings dating mainly from the eighteenth and nineteenth centuries. The whitewashed church of St James, dating from about 1150 but largely rebuilt in 1730, is situated on the Ireby road, one mile north-west of the village, at Uldale Mill. The surrounding countryside is unlike that of central Lakeland; there are gentle, rolling hills, lush pastures, unfenced roads, open moorland and no lakes – except for Over Water, Little Tarn and the Chapelhouse Reservoir. The River Ellen, which rises on the heathery moorland of Skiddaw Forest, flows to the south of Uldale and then north to Ireby, once an ancient market town. Although the farmers keep a few cattle, allowing them to graze on the rich pastures of the valley, their real livelihood – like that of most farmers in Lakeland – depends on sheep. Wild fell ponies can often be seen on the Uldale and Caldbeck Fells.

THIRLMERE
from Wythburn

'Manchester,' Ruskin wrote to *The Times* in October 1877, 'is plotting to steal the waters of Thirlmere and the clouds of Helvellyn.' He was one of many eminent figures who protested vehemently against the proposal by Manchester Corporation to pipe water from Thirlmere to the urban areas of south Lancashire, nearly 100 miles away. The Thirlmere Defence Association was hurriedly formed to prevent the scheme, but in 1879, despite a long and bitterly fought campaign, Parliament ruled in favour of the reservoir, and Manchester Corporation was given the official authority to purchase the land and start construction. A dam was built at the northern end of what was then two small lakes and the water level raised by 54 feet. The ancient village and farmsteads of Wythburn were submerged, including the Cherry Tree Inn and Armboth House. Wythburn Church, built in 1640 and restored in 1872, was located higher up the valley and escaped the flooding.

STRIDING EDGE,
HELVELLYN

At 3,118 feet above sea-level, Helvellyn is the third highest mountain in England, only 44 feet lower than Scafell and 88 feet lower than Scafell Pike. The view towards the north-east from its lofty summit looks down on Striding Edge, a place that struck terror into the hearts of early writers. Wainwright regards it as 'the finest ridge there is in Lakeland, for walkers – its traverse is always an exhilarating adventure in fair weather or foul, and can be made easy or difficult according to choice.' On their 'Pikteresk Toor' of 1799, Coleridge was introduced to Helvellyn by Wordsworth and, after he had moved to the Lakes, he climbed it many times and, on one occasion, by moonlight! Sir Walter Scott also climbed 'the dark brow of Helvellyn' and saw that 'Striden-edge round Red-Tarn was bending'. In the photograph, almost hidden behind Striding Edge, is Red Tarn with Ullswater in the distance.

WHELPSIDE GILL, THIRLMERE

Situated near the foot of Whelpside Gill, which runs into Thirlmere, is the long, low chapel of Wythburn (called by Wordsworth a 'modest house of prayer'), the starting-point for the popular 'Wythburn' route, via Birk Side, up Helvellyn. It stands hidden in trees by the busy Keswick to Kendal road. The remains of the famous 'Rock of Names' used to stand one mile to the north, just beyond the castellated water-pumping station called Straining Well. The upright block of stone was a favourite meeting-spot, between Keswick and Grasmere, for Coleridge, the two Hutchinson sisters and the Wordsworths – and on it they carved their names. Canon Rawnsley tried to save it before the valley was flooded but found it impossible to move. The rock was blown up when the new road was built and the fragments were collected and cemented together. It was moved from Thirlmere in 1984 and re-erected behind the Wordsworth Museum, Grasmere.

LOWTHWAITE FARM, ST JOHN'S IN THE VALE

St John's in the Vale lies two and a half miles east of Keswick and immediately north of Thirlmere, delightfully situated between the northernmost fells of the massive Helvellyn range and the long, isolated ridge of High Rigg. At the foot of Clough Head is Lowthwaite Farm, standing with its back to the screes which rise over 500 feet up the fell to Fisher Wife's Rake. St John's in the Vale is linked to the valley of the Naddle Beck by a small pass – running between High Rigg and Low Rigg – on the top of which is the church of St John, from which the vale gets its name. At the south-east end of the valley, on the western slopes of Watson's Dodd, is Castle Rock. From a distance, according to legend, the rock appears to be an enchanted castle, with towers, walls and buttresses. But, when approached, it turns back into a heap of rubble. It is more popularly known as the Castle Rock of Triermain and was described by Sir Walter Scott in his Arthurian poem *The Bridal of Triermain*.

LAUNCHY GILL,
THIRLMERE

The clear waters of Launchy Gill rise on the southern extremities of Armboth Fell and gather in Launchy Tarn, before rushing down the craggy eastern slopes into Thirlmere. On the southern bank of the gill, a steep track descends, past some spectacular waterfalls, into a dark forest of conifers. They were planted by Manchester Corporation and conceal traces of 'old' Thirlmere – overgrown cart-tracks, crumbling dry-stone walls, ruined farmhouses and abandoned huts – which survive from before the valley was flooded to form a reservoir. Less than a mile to the north of Launchy Gill, and submerged beneath the waters of the reservoir, lies Armboth House, once reputed to be 'the haunt of the grisliest set of phantoms' in Lakeland. According to legend, once a year on the eve of Hallowe'en, the dismembered spirits of unavenged murder victims gather at the house. A monkey-puzzle tree, which once stood in the grounds of the house, still grows on the shore above the water-line and marks the site of the submerged house.

FISHERCRAG PLANTATION,
THIRLMERE

'O Thirlmere!' wrote Coleridge in 1803, 'let me somehow or other celebrate the world in thy mirror – Conceive all possible varieties of Form, Fields, & Trees, and naked or ferny Crags – ravines, behaired with Birches – Cottages, smoking chimneys, dazzling wet places of small rock-precipices – all these, within a divine outline in a mirror of three miles distinct vision!' Almost ninety years later the valley was flooded by Manchester Corporation to form a reservoir, and the Thirlmere of the Lake Poets vanished forever. The lake (or two lakes as there were then) grew from two and a half miles to nearly four miles in length, and the width was increased, at its widest point, from 600 to 700 yards. The lower slopes of the surrounding fells were planted with conifers but, although the now mature trees are far from ugly, Thirlmere – with its dark pine forests reflected in the still expanse of water – somehow appears to belong to some other place, rather than to Lakeland.

KENDAL & THE EASTERN LAKES

HOWE GRAIN VALLEY,
MARTINDALE

The valleys of Ramps Gill and Bannerdale are separated by a 1,887-foot-high wedge of fell known as The Nab, which lies entirely within the private, walled boundaries of the Martindale Deer Forest. Here can be found not only herds of red deer but also wild fell ponies. The photograph was taken from Howe Grain, looking south towards the head of the Ramps Gill valley and the snow-capped ridge of the High Street range. Wordsworth describes the valley in his guide to the Lakes and, over 150 years later, the scene has hardly changed: 'Towards its head, this valley splits into two parts; and in one of these (that to the left) there is no house, nor any building to be seen but a cattle-shed on the side of a hill . . . A few old trees remain, relics of the forest, a little stream hastens, though with serpentine windings, through the uncultivated hollow, where many cattle were pasturing. . . .'

In the centuries following the Norman Conquest, the farmers living around the periphery of Lakeland found themselves caught up in the turbulent warfare between Scotland and England. Scottish raiders frequently made incursions into the region and, without the protection of a castle or an armed guard, the farmers were considered easy targets: their homes were burnt, their animals stolen and their women raped.

After the great Scottish victory over the English at the Battle of Bannockburn in 1314, the raids from across the Border became so frequent and so ferocious that the wealthier landowners were forced to build 'pele towers'. These strong defensive structures are unique to the north of England and can be found in all the counties along the Border, but more have been preserved in Cumbria than anywhere else. Strictly speaking the 'pele' or 'peel' refers to the walled defensive yard around the tower and is derived from *pilum*, meaning 'stake' or 'palisade'. Most of the pele towers in Cumbria – and there are around ninety in all – date from the fourteenth and fifteenth centuries, although they continued to be built right up until the beginning of the seventeenth century, long after the Scottish raids had ceased.

The walls of a typical pele tower are between four and ten feet thick, with a few small slits for windows and an entrance on the first floor (reached by a ladder which could be pulled up in times of danger). It was built in the shape of a massive stone rectangle and contained three storeys: a vaulted storage area on the ground floor, which could accommodate animals; a hall and kitchen on the floor above; and, on the top floor, a space for living and sleeping. In addition, there was access to the battlemented roof for look-out and defensive purposes. The tower was surrounded by a high wall, forming a courtyard in which the animals could also be kept. In more peaceful times a hall was added and subsequently – with further modifications and extensions over the centuries – the pele tower came to be incorporated into many of Lakeland's beautiful manor houses, including Levens Hall, Sizergh Castle, Dalemain and Muncaster Castle.

The less wealthy farmers, however, were unable to afford the protection of a pele tower and, when the alarm was sounded to warn them that raiders were on their way, they fled with their families and livestock up into the fells. Their houses were timber-framed, with walls made of wattle and daub, clay, turf or roughly piled stones. None of these dwellings were permanent and none have survived intact.

It was not until the mid-seventeenth century that the farmhouses and cottages began to be constructed in the form and style which is now considered to be the traditional domestic architecture of Lakeland. These buildings are entirely functional – without ornamentation – and are built solidly and simply, using locally quarried stone and possessing a rugged quality which blends in perfectly with the surrounding landscape of the fells. This characteristic style persisted for about two hundred years until the mid-nineteenth century, when builders, influenced by national standards of construction, began to use non-local materials and adopt more fashionable styles.

The traditional farmhouse was built 'back-side to wind' and was sited to take full advantage of the natural shelter and protection of the surrounding hills and trees. It was designed to a basic plan, which consisted of two units: the 'down house', or working area, and the 'fire house', or living area, with a passage, or 'hallan', dividing them. The central front door led into the hallan and, at the far end of the passage, facing doors opened into the two main downstairs rooms: one directly into the down house and the other, by way of a short passage, into the fire house. As the farmers became more settled and prosperous they added extensions and wings to this basic pattern. Townend, the Troutbeck home of the Browne family, is an excellent example of a Lakeland yeoman farmer's house, with tall cylindrical chimneys, slate roof and lime-rendered stonework.

Many of the families in the region were involved in the wool industry and, inevitably, this influenced the construction of their cottages, farms and barns. A typical feature is the wooden 'spinning gallery', where the wool was either spun or hung out to dry. It also served as a storage area and a means of access to the upper floor of the building. Most spinning galleries are located on the north and east side of the building: some form part of the outbuildings, as at Yew Tree Farm, Coniston; while others form part of the farmhouse itself, as at Thorn House, Low Hartsop, in the eastern Lakes.

Many of the houses in Lakeland are whitewashed or colour washed, although Wordsworth hated the fashion which was then becoming common. He recommended that if a house must be painted then it should be painted to blend in with the landscape, and not 'materially impair the majesty of a mountain'.

SIZERGH CASTLE,
KENDAL

Sizergh Castle, three miles south of Kendal, has been the seat of the Stricklands since 1239, and, even though the property was granted to the National Trust in 1950 and is today regularly open to the public, Sizergh still remains their home. Standing beside a small lake amidst beautiful parkland, it is one of the finest fortified houses in Cumbria. The oldest part of the building is the massive, mid-fourteenth-century pele tower, almost 60 feet high. The adjoining Great Hall was built in about 1450 and a central block and two long wings were added during the Elizabethan period. Parts of the building were remodelled, however, in the second half of the eighteenth century. The house contains early English and French furniture, portraits, silver, china, Jacobean relics, Tudor panelling and seventeenth-century Flemish tapestry. The finest feature of the garden is the magnificent limestone rockery which contains one of the largest collections of ferns in Britain.

HOLY TRINITY CHURCH, KENDAL

Formerly known as Kirkby Kendal, meaning 'the village with a church in the valley of the River Kent', Kendal is a large and important town on the south-east fringe of the National Park. Its houses, built mostly of the local grey limestone, straddle both sides of the River Kent, running parallel to it for more than two miles. 'The Auld Grey Town' was granted its market charter at the end of the twelfth century and, after Flemish weavers were imported in 1331, it became a major centre for the production of a heavy woollen cloth known as 'Kendal Green'. The Latin motto on the town's coat of arms means 'wool is my bread'. Dating from the thirteenth century, the wool church of the Holy Trinity is one of the largest parish churches in England, with no fewer than five aisles. It was extensively restored in the mid-nineteenth century and is pleasantly situated on the west bank of the river. Abbot Hall, a large house built in 1759, stands in a park near the church and contains a Museum of Lakeland Life and Industry.

KENDAL CASTLE, KENDAL

Dominating the important market town of Kendal, the stark, grey ruins of Kendal Castle stand on a small glacial mound overlooking the Kent valley. Wordsworth called it 'a stern castle mouldering on the brow of a green hill'. It was built in the twelfth century and is famous for being the birthplace of Catherine Parr, the sixth and last wife of Henry VIII. After the death of Catherine's brother in 1571, leaving no heirs to claim it, the castle was abandoned and fell into decay. It was acquired for the town in 1896 to mark the diamond jubilee of Queen Victoria and is now surrounded by a public park. Kendal, unusually, possesses two castles: Kendal Castle, on the east side of the River Kent and, on the west, the more ancient motte and bailey Castle Howe. Known also as The Mount, Castle Howe is surmounted by an obelisk commemorating the Glorious Revolution of 1688, when James II was deposed and William of Orange and his wife Mary jointly assumed the throne.

LEVENS HALL, KENDAL

Situated on the edge of the National Park, five miles south of Kendal, Levens Hall is one of the largest Elizabethan houses in Cumbria. Originally built in the latter half of the thirteenth century, it incorporates a medieval pele tower and the hall attached to it. The property was sold to Alan Bellingham in 1562. After his death, in about 1580, his son James inherited the estate. During the Elizabethan period, as a result of increased wealth and prosperity, many mansions were rebuilt, and Bellingham followed the trend by completely remodelling the old house to create a property that is unique. The bay window (shown in the photograph), like the rest of the drawing room, has a plaster ceiling decorated with an eight-pointed star and little pendants. Levens Hall, with its fine collection of Jacobean furniture, richly carved oak panelling, plasterwork, paintings, tapestries and leather wall-hangings, is now the treasured home of the Bagot family.

LEVENS HALL, KENDAL

The topiary garden at Levens Hall is considered to be the best example of its kind in the world. It was designed by Monsieur Guillaume Beaumont, gardener to King James II, who helped to design the garden at Hampton Court. Laid out in 1692, it is beautifully maintained in its original plan with colourful annual bedding. For the topiary Beaumont used yew and beech, with box forming the borders of the beds. The trees are clipped annually, a job which normally takes from mid-September to Christmas. The park at Levens, described by Thomas West in his *Guide to the Lakes* (1780) as 'the sweetest spot that fancy can imagine', is now separated from the house and its harmonious gardens by the main road (A6) to Kendal. The River Kent winds through the hundred-acre park, which is well stocked with black fallow deer and contains a noble, mile-long avenue of ancient oaks. Today there is also a working collection of steam engines at Levens Hall, as well as a gift shop, a children's play area, and a picnic area.

TOWNEND, TROUTBECK

Nestling in the shelter of the fellside above the Trout Beck valley, Townend is an excellent example of a Lakeland yeoman farmer's house, with tall cylindrical chimneys, slate roof, oak-mullioned windows and lime-rendered stonework. It is based on the typical plan of a long hall, or hallan, with an attached kitchen, or down house, on one side and a living room, or fire house, on the other. The oldest part of the present building is probably the central main living room, believed to have been built in the late sixteenth or early seventeenth century. Further improvements were made to the farmhouse in the eighteenth century. The wool barn with its spinning gallery (on the opposite side of the road) was used to store the fleeces. Now part of Townend Farm, the barn is still in agricultural use today. Townend is situated about one mile south of Troutbeck village and just over two miles south-east of Ambleside. It is owned by the National Trust and is open to the public.

TOWNEND, TROUTBECK

For over four centuries the Brownes, who were wealthy yeoman farmers, lived in the solid stone farmhouse at Townend and, in so doing, they literally carved their place in history. In most of the rooms the oak panelling and furniture has been elaborately carved by one member of the family or another and then dated and initialled. In the kitchen, or down house (shown in the photograph), the small child's chair by the fireplace bears the initials 'K.M.B.' (standing for Katharine Margaret Browne) and the date '1873'; it was made by the last George Browne (1834–1914). Standing against the wall to the left of the hearth is a beautiful range of built-in carved oak furniture, including boxes, cupboards, drawers, shelves and even a grandfather clock. The cupboard, its door decorated with spindles and inscribed 'T.H. 1770', was used to store food. The kitchen, with its slate floor, was probably built shortly after the marriage of George Browne and Susannah Rawlinson in 1623.

LOW WOOD,
HARTSOP VALLEY

The road north-east from Ambleside joins the main Windermere–Ullswater road high on Kirkstone Pass, and – once over the 1,489-foot-high summit – descends to Brothers Water and the Hartsop Valley. The Wordsworths often walked the route from Ambleside to Patterdale, and in 1802, on their way home to Grasmere, Wordsworth stopped north of Brothers Water to rest and compose a poem. Dorothy later wrote in her *Journal*: 'I left William sitting on the bridge, and went along the path on the right side of the Lake through the wood. I was delighted with what I saw. The water under the boughs of the bare old trees, the simplicity of the mountains, and the exquisite beauty of the path.' Low Wood, a mixed woodland of oak, ash and hazel, drops down to the western shore of the Brothers Water, and has been designated a Site of Special Scientific Interest by the Nature Conservancy Council.

BROTHERS WATER,
HARTSOP VALLEY

Brothers Water is sometimes classed as 'the sixteenth lake' instead of Elterwater. Once called Broad Water, it is traditionally said to have received its present name when two brothers were drowned in its waters. In about 1785, while ice-skating, two more brothers 'did meet that melancholy fate'. 'It is remarkable,' Dorothy Wordsworth commented, 'that two pairs of brothers should have been drowned in that lake.' Brothers Water, lying two miles south of Patterdale, was probably once part of a much larger lake that also included Ullswater, until it was separated by silt and debris washed down from the surrounding fells.

The Hartsop Valley around Brothers Water is well-cultivated, with rich woodland growing on the lower slopes of the enclosing fells. The village of Hartsop nestles in the valley to the north-east of the tarn, and contains a few seventeenth-century farm buildings and a cluster of attractive stone cottages, some with spinning galleries. Hartsop means 'the valley of the deer'.

AIRA FORCE,
ULLSWATER

'There is, on the western side of Ullswater,' wrote Thomas De Quincey in his *Recollections of the Lake Poets*, 'a fine cataract (or, in the language of the country, a force) known by the name of Airey Force; and it is of importance enough, especially in rainy seasons, to attract numerous visitors from among "the Lakers".' Aira Force, as it is now known, is probably the most popular waterfall in Lakeland. From High Force, further up the gorge, Aira Beck tumbles down the rocks to pass beneath a stone footbridge, where – as Aira Force – it plunges 70 feet into a deep, wooded glen. The waterfall is said to be the scene of the tragic legend of Emma and Sir Eglamore, on which Wordsworth based his poem *The Somnambulist*.

ULLSWATER

Ullswater is characteristically a lake of ever-changing moods. In 1769 Thomas Gray noted that the lake was 'majestic in its calmness, clear and smooth as a blew mirror'. In his guide to the Lakes Wordsworth wrote that 'the lake, clouds, and mists were all in motion to the sound of sweeping winds.' Second only in size to Windermere, Ullswater is seven and a half miles long, about three quarters of a mile wide and over 200 feet deep. It is a serpentine lake with its head in the rugged mountainous rocks of the Borrowdale volcanic group, its middle in the low-lying slate of the Skiddaw group and its foot in the rounded hills of the Mell Fell conglomerate. Beyond, in the flat plain of the River Eamont, which flows out of the northern end of the lake, a belt of carboniferous limestone stretches north-eastwards towards Penrith. Its three distinct reaches, therefore, mark the gradual transitions from wild mountain scenery to gentler and less spectacular countryside. As Wordsworth remarked, Ullswater is 'perhaps, upon the whole, the happiest combination of beauty and grandeur which any of the Lakes affords'.

ST ANDREW'S CHURCHYARD, DACRE

Four miles south-west of Penrith and on the edge of the National Park, Dacre is an attractive village situated on high ground above the Dacre Beck. Its castle, built around a pele tower (like most Cumbrian castles), dates from the early fourteenth century. These fortified buildings were primarily the farmsteads of the lesser gentry and were constructed to protect the household, their livestock and their food against Scottish raiders. Later, in more peaceful times, a hall was added to the tower. The Norman church of St Andrew, its west tower rebuilt in 1810, is located to the north of the castle. It was built on the site of an ancient monastery, mentioned by the Venerable Bede, and excavations around the church have revealed some Anglo-Saxon artefacts and traces of a timber building, a drainage system and a cemetery. Standing in long grass, one in each corner of St Andrew's churchyard, are four great stone bears, of unknown origin. Pevsner suggests, however, that they may possibly have come from the former gatehouse of the castle.

DALEMAIN, POOLEY BRIDGE

The historic manor house of Dalemain, with its impressive Georgian front of local pink sandstone, stands in richly wooded parkland, one and a half miles north of Pooley Bridge, near the confluence of the Dacre Beck and the River Eamont. It has been the home of the Hasell family for over 300 years, since 1679, when Sir Edward Hasell purchased the estate. The oldest part of the present building is the Norman pele tower, to which the medieval hall was later added. The wings were built in the reign of Queen Elizabeth I and the Georgian facade erected in 1745. The interior contains fine oak panelling, Chinese hand-painted wallpaper, numerous paintings and portraits, beautiful period furniture and many other articles of interest. The mounted red deer heads come from Martindale Forest, which still belongs to the estate, covering about 30,000 acres to the east and south of Ullswater. Dalemain is open to the public and offers a rich variety of attractions.

ST MARTIN'S CHURCH, MARTINDALE

Wordsworth and Dorothy made a one-day excursion to Martindale in November 1805 and in his guide to the Lakes he describes the journey from Ullswater 'to the village (if village it may be called, for the houses are few, and separated from each other) a sequestered spot, shut out from the view of the lake. Crossed the one-arched bridge, below the chapel, with its "bare ring of mossy wall," and single yew-tree.' The chapel to which he refers is the old church of St Martin, standing at the entrance to Bannerdale in Howe Grain valley. It is one of two churches in Martindale: the newer one, St Peter's, is situated high up on top of The Hause, between Martindale and Howtown. It was built in 1882 to replace St Martin's, which by then had fallen into disrepair. The old church had been built in 1633 on the site of an earlier building dating back to the fourteenth century. St Martin's has now been restored and services are still held there during the summer months.

HIGH STREET from Racecourse Hill

The road linking the Roman forts at Galava (Ambleside) and Brocavum (Brougham, near Penrith) climbs high onto the eastern fells and runs along the long whale-backed crest of High Street (approximately 2,700 feet above sea-level). Although it is the highest Roman road in Britain, the route – called *Brettestrete*, 'the Britons' road', in the thirteenth century – was probably in use long before the arrival of the Romans. The ancient road is still clearly defined and is now a footpath. High Street refers not only to the flat, grassy ridge – where a crumbling dry-stone wall snakes its way along the top for miles – but also to the summit (2,718 feet). Until the early nineteenth century, the smooth, verdant top of High Street was the venue of the annual Mardale Shepherds' meet, with horse racing, wrestling, fell running and other sporting events amongst the attractions. Originally a gathering where the shepherds could retrieve or identify any stray sheep, it later became a great festive occasion.

SMALL WATER AND HAWESWATER from Nan Bield Pass

From Kentmere to Haweswater an old pack-horse route climbs to Nan Bield Pass (2,100 feet). The view from here looking north-east encompasses an attractive tarn, called Small Water, and Mardale, where the drowned village of Mardale Green lies beneath the waters of Haweswater Reservoir. (In the photograph Small Water is the nearest stretch of water with Haweswater beyond). Small Water's larger neighbour, Blea Water (at 207 feet the deepest tarn in Lakeland) lies less than half a mile to the north-west. The perpendicular cliffs on its western side rise hundreds of feet to High Street. It was over this precipice in about 1762 that a man named Dixon, while chasing a fox, is said to have plunged. Landing on the screes far below, he is reputed to have got up, pointed after the fox and shouted to the horrified onlookers, 'It's gone o'er theer, it's gone o'er theer!' before promptly falling down dead. In another version of the story he survives, without a broken bone!

HAYESWATER

A large and lonely tarn – surrounded on three sides by a steep wall of fells – Hayeswater lies in the Hayeswater Gill valley, two miles east of Brothers Water. At 1,383 feet above sea-level, it is dammed at its northern end and is used as a reservoir to supply water to Penrith, twelve miles north-east. To the south-east of the tarn the western slopes of High Street rise over 1,000 feet to the Roman road which runs along its flat, grassy ridge. The Knott and Gray Crag overlook Hayeswater to the east and west respectively. Beyond The Knott is Kidsty Pike (2,560 feet), a distinctive peak with its eastern slopes dropping down to the Haweswater reservoir. Hayeswater can be approached from the village of Hartsop by taking the pleasant track which follows the Hayeswater Gill up the valley. The golden eagle has returned to this wild and remote area, and herds of red deer often come down off the high fells to feed on the rough grass and drink from the clear waters of the tarn.

SHAP ABBEY, SHAP

The ruins of the Abbey of St Mary lie on the banks of the River Lowther, high on the eastern fells, in a remote and sheltered limestone valley to the west of the village of Shap. Thomas, son of Gospatric, a Westmorland baron, granted the land to the Order of Premonstratensian monks at the very end of the twelfth century. The Order was intended for those monks who wished to combine the life of prayer and discipline with parish work as priests, serving local communities. The Premonstratensian monks were known as 'white canons' because of the colour of their habits. In 1540, at the Dissolution, the abbey lands were sold and some of the buildings were converted into a farm (which is still in use). The rest had their roofs removed and were allowed to decay. Today little remains, except for the foundations, a few doorways and walls and the early sixteenth-century west tower. Shap Abbey is now in the care of English Heritage.

HAWESWATER from High Loup

Having converted Thirlmere into a reservoir Manchester Corporation made plans to do the same with Haweswater. In 1919, through the Haweswater Act, they were given the necessary authority, although it was not until the 1930s that work on the construction of the main dam began. In 1940 the valley was flooded and the level of Haweswater raised by 96 feet, thereby increasing the lake from two-and-a-half miles in length to four, and from 102 feet in depth to 198. The village of Mardale Green now lies submerged under Haweswater. In times of severe drought the water-level can drop dramatically, and the remains of the village are revealed. Except on these rare occasions, the level of the water remains fairly constant but never fixed, and this inevitable fluctuation in level produces a white tide line around the perimeter of the lake. The valley lies to the east of the High Street range and can only be approached by road from the north-east.

WINDERMERE & THE SOUTHERN LAKES

BOWNESS BAY,
BOWNESS-ON-WINDERMERE

Bowness-on-Windermere, Lakeland's most popular holiday resort, is an excellent centre for boating activities. Throughout the season, steamers operate from the pier in Bowness Bay, and there is a regular ferry service across the lake to the Hawkshead road. Situated in the middle reaches of the east shore of Windermere, opposite Belle Isle, Bowness seems more like a seaside resort (without the amusement arcades) than an inland town. It is older than Windermere town to the north-east, with which it is now joined, and dates from at least Anglo-Saxon times. Today the houses and hotels in Bowness are essentially Victorian, built to cater for the sudden influx of new residents and tourists after 1847, when the railway line to Windermere was opened. The church of St Martin, consecrated in 1483 and restored in 1870, contains a beautiful fifteenth-century stained-glass window.

For at least 7,000 years, since the arrival of the first settlers, farming has been the principal occupation in Lakeland. Apart from those fortunate enough to acquire or inherit the rich soil of the valleys, the inhabitants have had to work land which is, on the whole, poor, with living made even more difficult by mountainous terrain and unfavourable weather conditions. Using knowledge and experience accumulated over centuries, the farmers have endeavoured to overcome these environmental limitations by hill farming, rearing cattle and, more particularly, sheep.

The breed of mountain sheep traditional to Lakeland is the Herdwick, a small but extremely hardy animal, able to withstand even the harshest winters on the fells. There are various theories about the Herdwick's origin: the most popular suggests that the breed is descended from a number of animals washed ashore from a wrecked ship, either in Viking or Elizabethan times. It would seem, however, that they almost certainly predate the Elizabethan period by several centuries – for it is recorded that the monks of Furness Abbey had 'Herdwyk' farms. Some authorities have even argued that the sheep date from the Bronze Age or even Neolithic times.

After the conquest the Normans established a number of important monasteries, endowing them with huge tracts of land. The monks of Furness Abbey, which was the second wealthiest Cistercian house in England at the time of the Dissolution, owned nearly all of southern Lakeland with land in Borrowdale to the north, and Eskdale to the west as well. It was the medieval monks who turned farming into an industry. They not only exploited the rock and mineral wealth of Lakeland but – by clearing the forest in order to make charcoal, which was essential for the smelting of iron ore – created pastures for their cattle and sheep as well. Although they also developed fisheries on Coniston Water and Windermere, their greatest contribution to the region was the establishment of the wool trade, an industry which brought prosperity to Lakeland and continued to flourish long after the monasteries had been dissolved.

For most of the small farmers, however – unlike the great landowners – life was hard and in order to survive they were forced to supplement their meagre incomes by spinning wool in their homes. Attached to many farms and outbuildings were timber-built 'spinning galleries'; a few have survived, notably at Yew Tree Farm, Coniston, Troutbeck and Low Hartsop.

It was not just the thin acid soils of the fells, or the rough terrain and poor climatic conditions, which caused problems for the farmers. Right up until the beginning of the seventeenth century, the region was a prime target for raiders and rustlers from across the Scottish border. Although those living in the more remote areas of central Lakeland may have been left alone, those on the periphery lived in constant fear of attack. Most of the hill farmers had an arable field in which a few crops could be grown. Primarily, however, their existence depended on sheep and, if their animals were stolen or if their entire flock succumbed to disease, they could eventually have to face extreme hardship, even starvation.

A traditional Lakeland farm is sited just above the valley floor on the sheltered, lower slopes of the fellside, near a stream for water and possibly a tarn or lake for fish. Uncleared woodland supplies timber for buildings and wood for fires; while the peat bogs provide an additional source of fuel. Rock and stone is readily available for the construction of dry-stone walls, farmhouses and barns (most of the stone buildings which survive today were built after 1650). Enclosures for the animals are sited around the farmhouse and stretch up the slopes of the valley sides, while the high open fells above are available for common grazing. In the valley bottoms there are small meadows for hay and pastures for cattle. In the past the farmer would have kept dairy cows, but now it is beef cattle which predominate. However, the Lakeland economy today is still based on sheep.

The National Trust considers that the maintenance of the farming system is inseparable from the preservation of the landscape. As the largest landowner in the National Park (looking after over eighty working farms and owning 30,000 sheep), it is dedicated to the repair, restoration and maintenance of the fell farms. Working in partnership with its tenants, the Trust recognises that – even with Government subsidies – the income from hill farming is not very great and, without help, farms can go out of business. Many farmers supplement their income during the tourist season by taking in paying guests and this is encouraged, providing it does not conflict with the Trust's prime objectives of farming and landscape preservation.

DUDDON VALLEY
from near High Tongue

The road winding south through Dunnerdale below High Tongue leaves the valley of the River Duddon and enters the valley of the Tarn Beck. Tarn Beck is a sizeable stream and for over two miles runs parallel to the Duddon – from which it is separated by a barrier of rocky 'tongues' – before joining the river at Seathwaite (not to be confused with the Seathwaite in Borrowdale). The small farming community, surrounded by fells, is associated with the Reverend Robert Walker, who was the curate of Seathwaite from 1735 to 1802. Wordsworth refers in several poems to the 'Wonderful' Walker, 'whose good works formed an endless retinue'. He was a remarkable man who lived with a large family on a small income; he not only served as pastor at Seathwaite church for sixty-six years, but also taught the local children, laboured in the fields, made his own clothes and acted as the community's physician and scribe. He and his wife lie buried in the churchyard.

BELLE ISLE,
WINDERMERE

Formerly known as Long Holm, Belle Isle was named after Isabella Curwen, the teenage heiress to Workington Hall and the Curwen estates, who purchased the 38-acre island and its house in 1781. It is the largest of Windermere's fourteen islands and is situated in the shallower middle reaches of the lake, opposite Bowness-on-Windermere, from where it can be reached by a ferry. Belle Isle, over half a mile long, is the lake's only inhabited island and has a unique Georgian round house. It was built on the site of a Roman villa in 1774 by John Plaw for a Mr English, who was severely criticized for his awful taste. Described by Wordsworth in *The Prelude* as a 'pepper pot', the domed house forms a perfect circle, 54 feet in diameter, with a portico, supported by slender columns, over the front door. Despite its seemingly small size, it contains twenty bedrooms, all of which connect as it has no corridors. The grounds were landscaped by Thomas White in the late 1780s.

WINDERMERE
from Wansfell

Windermere has been an important waterway for nearly two thousand years – at least since the time when the Romans occupied the fort of Galava at the head of the lake. Quarried stone, iron ore and charcoal have been shipped down the lake for centuries. During the nineteenth century industrial transport was superseded by pleasure craft, and today Windermere is a popular recreational centre for all sorts of boating activities and water sports. The lake – ten and a half miles long, one mile wide and 219 feet deep – is not only Lakeland's but also England's largest lake, although it is almost divided in the middle by Belle Isle. Windermere is named after a Norseman, Vinandr or Winland, and means Vinandr's lake. It is set amid beautifully wooded fells, and has a varied shoreline full of delightful little promontories and bays. Windermere town, once the village of Birthwaite, developed into a popular tourist centre when the railway line was opened in 1847.

CARTMEL PRIORY,
CARTMEL

The village of Cartmel (the name is derived from the Old Norse for 'the sandbank by the rocky ground') lies in the pleasant valley of the River Eea, two miles west of Grange-over-Sands. In 1185 'the land of Cartmel' was granted by King John to William Marshall, Earl of Pembroke, who, three years later, founded a priory of Augustinian canons on it. Cartmel Priory was demolished at the Dissolution and all that now remains is the fourteenth-century gatehouse and the priory church, which was saved because the local people claimed it as their parish church. The Preston family of nearby Holker Hall later acquired most of the priory estates, and in about 1620 the church was restored by George Preston. Further restoration work was carried out in the nineteenth century. The Cartmel estates subsequently passed by descent to the Lowthers and then to the Cavendishes, who still own them today. The gatehouse is now owned by the National Trust.

CONISTON WATER
from High Peel Near

Five and a quarter miles long, half a mile wide and 184 feet deep, Coniston Water is the third largest of the lakes and is dominated, to the west, by The Old Man of Coniston. The eastern side of the lake is heavily wooded with trees rising up onto moorland. There are two main islands on Coniston Water, both owned by the National Trust: Fir Island and Peel Island (shown in the photograph), which is 'Wild Cat Island' in Arthur Ransome's *Swallows and Amazons*. Anciently called Thurston Mere, the lake is long, narrow and straight and, in consequence, has often been used for attempts on the world water-speed record. On 4 January 1967, on his final run, Donald Campbell managed to reach 328 mph in the turbo-jet engined Bluebird K7. Although it was then the highest speed ever achieved on water, it could not be made official for, before he had completed the required distance, Bluebird crashed and Campbell was killed. His body has never been recovered.

BRANTWOOD, CONISTON

When John Ruskin bought Brantwood in 1871, without even seeing it, he discovered that he had purchased 'a mere shed of rotten timber and loose stone', but with, admittedly, 'on the whole, the finest view I know in Cumberland or Lancashire'. Repairs to the house, which was originally built in about 1797, were started in the autumn and he moved in the following year. The first addition was the bedroom turret, which had extensive views. He continued to extend the house and the estate over the years, adding a dining room, servants' quarters, stables, a coach house, a schoolroom, a nursery and a magnificent studio. The amount of land belonging to the house increased from the original purchase of 16 acres to around 500. Ruskin made Brantwood his home for the last twenty-nine years of his life, filling it with priceless art treasures. Today, the house, gardens and nature trails are open to the public.

CONISTON WATER from High Hollin Bank

Coniston, once an important mining centre, lies at the north-western end of Coniston Water and at the foot of the 2,633-foot-high fell known as The Old Man of Coniston. The rich copper veins in Coppermines Valley, above the village, are thought to have been mined from Roman times, but were evidently particularly productive from the sixteenth century. Although the slate quarries are still being worked, mining ceased in the early twentieth century. John Ruskin is buried in the churchyard at Coniston. Between 1860 and 1940 a steamboat operated up and down the lake; it was known as the 'Gondola', because of its long, curved prow and shallow design. Eighty-five feet long and able to carry over 200 passengers, it was converted into a houseboat and eventually sank in a storm in 1963. The National Trust have restored it to its original glory and 'Gondola' now offers a regular scheduled service.

BIRKS BRIDGE, DUDDON VALLEY

The River Duddon rises near the summit of Wrynose Pass and weaves a south-westerly course, through one of the loveliest valleys in Lakeland. It was one of Wordsworth's favourite rivers. 'The power of waters over the minds of Poets has been acknowledged from the earliest ages,' he wrote, and he was inspired to compose no less than thirty-four sonnets about it collected under the title *The River Duddon*.

> The struggling Rill
> insensibly is grown
> Into a Brook of loud and
> stately march,
> Crossed ever and anon by
> plank or arch.

Along its course the river is crossed by various methods: stepping stones, clapper bridges (slate slabs laid on boulders) and narrow pack-horse bridges. Birks Bridge (nearly two miles north of Seathwaite) is a fine example of the latter, built across a rock chasm on the edge of Dunnerdale Forest. It has small holes in the parapet to allow flood water through.

CATHEDRAL CAVE, TILBERTHWAITE

The route from Little Langdale to the 2,502-foot-high summit of Wetherlam crosses the River Brathay at Slater's Bridge, and climbs out of the valley towards High Tilberthwaite. In this wooded area the fellside is gashed and scarred by centuries of quarrying, during which, it is estimated, some three million cubic yards of slate were removed. Not far from the path is a tunnel in the fellside which unexpectedly opens into a huge and spectacular green cavern known as Cathedral Cave. Unlike most caverns it is lit by an opening at the side. The high, vaulted roof is supported by an impressive pillar of rock, below which the ground drops away into a dark and ominous pool. The slate that was taken from this vast cavern was hacked out by quarrymen (traditionally known as Old Men) who had to hang from the roof on chains. The fellside around here is honeycombed with old mine and quarry workings: many are extremely dangerous and entering them is not recommended.

DUDDON VALLEY
from Hardknott Pass

The River Duddon once formed the boundary between the old counties of Cumberland and Lancashire. On its twelve-mile-long journey through the Duddon Valley – or Dunnerdale as it is sometimes called – the river passes through wild, windswept grassland, dense conifer forest, dramatic gorges, lush meadows, ancient woodland, reed-filled marshland and treacherous mud-flats. From its source the infant river – for a distance of two and a half miles – follows part of the Roman military route across Lakeland, which linked the western port of Glannoventa (Ravenglass) to Galava (Ambleside). At Cockley Beck the old Roman road leaves the Duddon Valley and heads west, climbing the tortuous slopes of Hardknott and going over Hardknott Pass, past the Roman fort of Mediobogdum and down into Eskdale. From the pass there is a magnificent view looking down into Dunnerdale and across to the distant southern fells.

YEW TREE FARM,
CONISTON

Little is known about the farmhouses of Lakeland before the seventeenth century, for none remain intact. It is probable that most were constructed around a timber 'cruck' frame. Between about 1650 and 1750 many farmhouses were rebuilt in stone. Many families in Lakeland were involved in the wool industry during this period and, inevitably, this influenced the construction of their houses and farms. The open 'spinning gallery' became a typical feature, where the women and girls sometimes went to spin the wool, taking advantage of the daylight and fresh air. The gallery, however, was not solely used for spinning: it also served as a storage area, a place where the wool was hung up to dry and as a means of access to the upper floor of the building. Usually the gallery was built as part of the house but at Yew Tree Farm – one of eighty Lakeland hill farms protected by the National Trust – there is a fine example attached to the barn.

TARN HOWS, CONISTON

Tarn Hows is an artificial lake lying in wooded fell country just over two miles north-east of Coniston. This celebrated and extremely popular beauty spot is named after a nearby farm and was originally three swampy tarns, known as Monk Coniston Tarns or, simply, The Tarns. Strictly speaking, however, Tarn Hows refers to the 'hows', or hill, above the tarn. Around the close of the nineteenth century, the local landowner built a dam and created one large irregularly shaped tarn with two small islands. Much of the surrounding area was later planted with larch, spruce and pine which, against a backdrop of soaring fells, makes the half-mile-long tarn one of the prettiest in Lakeland. In 1930 Sir S. H. Scott presented it to the National Trust, who now have the difficult two-fold task of maintaining public access while trying to control the inevitable erosion caused by the huge numbers of visitors. It is strongly recommended, therefore, that Tarn Hows be avoided during the summer months.

ESTHWAITE WATER

Black Beck rises on Iron Keld (north-east of Tarn Hows) and flows south-eastwards, past Hawkshead Hall and the market town of Hawkshead, to enter Esthwaite Water at its marshy northern tip. Esthwaite Water simply means 'the lake by the eastern clearing', and at its southern end it is connected with Windermere by the Cunsey Beck. Near the head of the lake, and once part of it, is a small oval-shaped tarn known as the Priest's Pot. The name is a mystery, but the locals have two theories: the first is that a priest drowned there; the second refers to the pot and points to the fact that it holds about as much as a thirsty priest might drink if it were filled with ale. On the west shore of the lake is Esthwaite Hall where Edwin Sandys, the founder of Hawkshead Grammar School, was born in 1519. The lake is owned by the Esthwaite Estates which belong to his family. On the opposite shore to the Hall is Near Sawrey where Mrs Heelis, better known as Beatrix Potter, lived.

HAWKSHEAD GRAMMAR SCHOOL, HAWKSHEAD

Immediately below and to the south of the Parish Church of St Michael and All Saints is Hawkshead Grammar School, founded in 1585 by Edwin Sandys, a local man. Sandys was born at nearby Esthwaite Hall in 1519 and rose to prominence in the reign of Elizabeth I to become Bishop of Worcester and later Archbishop of York. The grammar school's most famous pupil was William Wordsworth, who was sent to study here after his mother's death. During term-time he lodged for a while at Anne Tyson's cottage in Hawkshead and later at Green End Cottage, Colthouse. Wordsworth attended the school from 1779 to 1787 and, encouraged by the headmaster, he began writing poems: indeed, his first known verses were written in 1785 to commemorate the school's two-hundredth anniversary. At one time the school had more than one hundred pupils, but it closed in 1909 and today houses a small museum and library.

HAWKSHEAD

In *The Prelude*, completed in 1805, Wordsworth describes the surrounding countryside and the small market town of Hawkshead, where as a boy he lived and went to school. Most of the buildings he knew are still standing: Anne Tyson's cottage where he lodged, the Old Grammar School and the fifteenth-century church of St Michael. Hawkshead lies in the vale of Esthwaite, near the head of Esthwaite Water, and contains an attractive muddle of timber-framed and whitewashed buildings, with squares linked by cobbled lanes, and courtyards and alleys often overhung by the upper floors of houses. It was once an important market town, but early in the nineteenth century its wool industry declined. It derives its name meaning 'the summer pastures of Haukr' from a Norseman who settled in the valley in the tenth century. Half a mile north of the village is Hawkshead Courthouse, once owned by the monks of Furness Abbey and now a National Trust folk museum.

ESTHWAITE WATER

As a schoolboy at Hawkshead Grammar School Wordsworth used to take early morning and evening walks around the shores of Esthwaite Water. On one occasion he saw, from the opposite bank, a pile of discarded clothes on the promontory of Strickland Ees; next day he discovered that they belonged to a schoolmaster who had drowned in the lake. Later he wrote of the experience in *The Prelude: Book V*:

> At length, the dead Man, 'mid that beauteous scene
> Of trees, and hills and water, bold upright
> Rose with his ghastly face; a spectre shape
> Of terror even! and yet no vulgar fear,
> Young as I was, a Child not nine years old,
> Possess'd me.

The lake, one and a half miles long and nearly half a mile wide, is shallow and rich in nutrients from the surrounding farmlands and human settlements. Animal and plant life is, therefore, plentiful.

HILL TOP, NEAR SAWREY

Beatrix Potter was born in London in 1866 and, when she was sixteen, her parents took her to Wray Castle for a holiday, where she became friends with the vicar, Canon H. Rawnsley. It was he who suggested that she should publish her first book *The Tale of Peter Rabbit*. It proved to be an enormous success and in 1905, with the royalties, she was able to buy Hill Top farm, in Near Sawrey, on the eastern side of Esthwaite Water. Increasing royalties enabled her to continue purchasing properties in the Lakes. In her will she bequeathed fourteen farms, numerous cottages and 4,000 acres of land to the National Trust. Hill Top is a typical seventeenth-century Westmorland Cottage of just six rooms, which can become extremely crowded at peak viewing times, especially during school and public holidays. However, during the spring, early summer or autumn, visitors will often find the place almost empty.

Ravenglass & the Western Lakes

HARDKNOTT ROMAN FORT, HARDKNOTT

The Romans built a military road through some of the highest and wildest country in England to link the two Roman forts of Galava (Ambleside) and Glannoventa (Ravenglass). From Ambleside the route – parts of which can still be traced – headed westwards, passing through Little Langdale, over the steep corkscrewing passes of Wrynose and Hardknott, down into Eskdale and along the valley to the sea. Near the summit of Hardknott Pass (1,291 feet), below the high rocky crags of Border End, they established one of the loneliest outposts in the whole of their Empire, calling it *Mediobogdum*, 'the fort in the middle of the bend', which describes its position in relation to the upper Esk valley. Hardknott Roman Fort, as it is known today, was built in the reign of the Emperor Hadrian (AD 117–138) and was designed to hold a cohort of about five hundred men.

Three or four thousand years after the last of the great ice-sheets had retreated north, Lakeland was covered by a vast primeval forest with only the highest mountain peaks projecting above the trees. The valley floors were water-logged swamps, with choking reeds and dense vegetation smothering everything, except where the water – much of it trapped in glacially-formed troughs and hollows – proved too deep for burrowing roots to gain a hold.

The west Cumbrian coast was inhabited by the first settlers from about 5,500 BC, a prehistoric people who had no knowledge of metals and depended on flint to make their implements and weapons. These Mesolithic groups of hunters and food-gatherers were the first to exploit the natural resources of the forest. But, although there is evidence that they burnt small areas of woodland to make clearings, their impact on the environment was minimal.

They were followed, in about 3,000 BC, by the Neolithic settlers, who as the first farmers brought about a major revolution in the way of life of early man. They penetrated deep into the heart of the Lakeland, clearing the hilltops of trees and also establishing axe-making factories high on the central fells. These finely sharpened and polished stone axes – which have been discovered throughout Britain – proved to be more efficient than the flint hand-axe of the Mesolithic people. When hafted it was a very effective tool, not only for felling the woodland but also for cultivating the land. In addition to growing crops and keeping livestock, they introduced the domestic arts of spinning, weaving and potting.

The arrival of the Bronze Age people, in about 1,500 BC, brought metallurgical skills to Cumbria and, with their far superior bronze axes and implements, the process of clearing the forest and tilling the soil was greatly accelerated. Because of the remoteness of Lakeland, the progression from one Age into the next was slower here than in other parts of Britain, especially the south; indeed, it is thought the Romans found the region still in the Bronze Age when they invaded in the first century AD.

The conquering legions built a supply port on the western coast at Glannoventa

(Ravenglass), including a fort and an adjoining Bath House, and systematically set about subjugating the hostile native Brigantes (a warlike, iron-using Celtic tribe who had arrived from the east in about 200 BC). For just over 300 years the Romans occupied Cumbria, building military roads and strategically sited forts. Yet, unlike all the other races who settled in the fells, they were never assimilated and always remained foreigners. In comparison with that of other conquerors, the influence of the Romans on the region was neither great nor lasting.

Sometime after the Roman withdrawal in about AD 410 the various Celtic tribes living in the north-west between the Clyde and the Mersey established the kingdom of Strathclyde. The inhabitants of this kingdom – which was enlarged to include Wales – were known as the *Cymru*, from which the names Cumberland and Cumbria are derived.

By the beginning of the seventh century AD the Anglo-Saxons – a mixed race of Germanic nations – had invaded, settling in all of east and north-east England. As the Celtic kingdom of Strathclyde began to disintegrate the Anglo-Saxons expanded westward and established settlements in Cumbria, most of which were confined to the fertile coastal plains of the western Lakes. There are a number of fine examples of beautifully preserved Anglian stone crosses in the area, such as the one still standing in the churchyard at Irton.

Since prehistoric times Lakeland has been settled by many different races. But the invaders who arrived in the ninth and tenth centuries AD proved in many ways to be the most important of all. These people were originally Vikings, but Vikings who had migrated to Ireland and the Isle of Man and from there had sailed to Cumbria. These Norsemen were sheep farmers and, instead of settling in the coastal areas, they sought out an environment similar to that of their traditional Scandinavian homeland – the fells and dales – which many of the other races had ignored.

They brought with them a culture and a way of life that was to endure all further conquests and, in the process, left a rich legacy of Norse words, which have been incorporated into the local language – *thwaite* (a clearing) as in Bassenthwaite, *tjorn* (a tarn), *dalr* (a dale or valley), *fjall* (a fell or mountain), *bekkr* (a beck or stream), and *fors* (a force or waterfall), to mention but a few of those that are most commonly found in the Lakes.

THE SUMMIT OF SCAFELL PIKE

At 3,210 feet above sea-level, Scafell Pike is not only the highest mountain in Lakeland but also the highest in England. Strictly speaking, Scafell Pike should be called Scafell Pikes, as it comprises three principal summits above 3,000 feet – Broad Crag (3,054 feet), Ill Crag (3,040 feet) and, the highest by at least 156 feet, Scafell Pike itself. There are a number of routes to the summit: from Wasdale Head; from Eskdale; from Great Langdale; and from Borrowdale, which offers a choice of two paths (one via Sty Head and the other via Esk Hause). All are long and arduous except from Wasdale Head. The area around the summit of Scafell Pike is extremely rough and barren, strewn with thousands of rocks of all shapes and sizes. The summit itself is marked by a massive circular stone cairn, with steps leading up onto a walled platform. The stone column in the foreground of the photograph is an Ordnance Survey Triangulation Station.

HERDWICK SHEEP, ESKDALE

The Herdwick, a hardy, white-faced, strong-boned sheep, has been a traditional part of Lakeland life for at least four hundred years. They are reputed to be descended from a number of sheep which were washed up on the Cumbrian coast either after the wreck of a Spanish galleon, at the time of the Spanish Armada, or from a Viking ship wrecked in the ninth or tenth century. The origin of the Herdwick may be obscure, but the breed is certainly Britain's hardiest sheep, staying out on the slopes of Lakeland's fells in summer and in winter. In order to identify the sheep of different farms, each farmer has his own mark, or 'smit'; a distinctive combination of a nick on the ear and a daub on the fleece, using a special coloured dye. The rams, which have curved horns and heavy manes, are locally known as 'tups' or, in central and western areas, 'tips'. Herdwick wool, which laid the foundations of the Lakeland wool trade, is strong and tough, but difficult to dye.

SWINSIDE STONE CIRCLE, NEAR BROUGHTON-IN-FURNESS

Swinside Stone Circle stands in a remote field, two miles to the west of Broughton-in-Furness and overlooking the Duddon estuary. Unlike Castlerigg, near Keswick, its location is undramatic and its existence is far less well known. In his notes on *Sonnet XVII*, Wordsworth mentioned that 'The country people call it *Sunken Church*'. And in the poem itself he referred to the stone circle as

> . . . that mystic Round of
> Druid frame
> Tardily sinking by its proper
> weight
> Deep into patient Earth,
> from whose smooth breast
> it came!

It forms an almost perfect circle, with a diameter of about 90 feet, and contains over fifty stones, but its purpose remains a mystery. It is thought to be of Bronze Age origin, over 3,500 years old, and consequently pre-dates the Druids by many hundreds of years. Although on private land, it can be viewed from a public footpath close by.

DEVOKE WATER, BIRKER FELL

Although Devoke Water is larger than Elterwater and about the same size as Rydal Water, it is classified as a tarn. Located on the moors of Birker Fell, between Eskdale and Dunnerdale, it occupies a site that has been described as bleak, austere, desolate, grim and even beautiful. Devoke Water – the name means 'the dark one' – is all of these and more, taking its varying moods from the weather. The present moorland was once covered by dense forest – over 7,000 years ago – but it was cleared by Neolithic farmers. Today the area around the black and shaley shores of Devoke Water is covered with literally hundreds of prehistoric remains, which almost certainly date back to the Bronze Age and include burial mounds, cairns, stone circles, settlements and field systems. Just over one mile south-west of the tarn are the 'ruins' of the legendary ancient city of Barnscar. At the eastern end of the tarn is a small stone boat-house and fishing lodge.

ESKDALE from Hardknott

The old Roman road from the fort at Ambleside to the port of Ravenglass passed through Little Langdale and over the steep hairpin passes of Wrynose and Hardknott before descending into the valley of the River Esk. The river rises near Esk Hause which, at 2,490 feet, is the highest foot-pass in Lakeland. The pass forms part of a huge amphitheatre of towering fells that dominate the rocky wilderness at the head of the valley. These include the Scafell range, Esk Pike, Bowfell and Crinkle Crags. Eskdale, which has no lake, stretches some thirteen miles westwards to the coast at Ravenglass where its river is joined by the Mite and the Irt. It is a beautiful valley containing a variety of landscape: from the rocky grandeur of the fells to the green meadows and woodlands of the plain and the sandy mud-flats of the estuary. It is also famous for its miniature railway which once transported iron ore and granite from the local mines and quarries to the coast.

STANLEY GHYLL FORCE,
DALEGARTH

The narrow-gauge Ravenglass to Eskdale Railway terminates at Dalegarth Station near Boot and, a short distance further south, on the opposite side of the River Esk, is Stanley Ghyll Force. It can be reached either from the riverside church of St Catherine or from Dalegarth Hall, where a mile-long path climbs up through a heavily wooded ravine to the falls. Named after the Stanleys, who once lived at Dalegarth Hall, Stanley Ghyll Force was a popular attraction in Victorian times when waterfalls were highly fashionable. Baddeley regarded it as 'the finest of its kind in Lakeland', adding that 'it is neither the height nor the volume of water which constitutes the attraction, but the setting.' Rising on the rough moorland of Birker Fell, the waters of the Stanley Ghyll pour north into a narrow gorge to plunge down more than 160 feet in a series of three vertical cascades, the highest dropping 37 feet into a deep pool, overhung with tall trees.

ESKDALE CORN MILL,
BOOT

An attractive hamlet, lying in the valley of the Whillan Beck where it enters Eskdale, Boot is surrounded by rocky crags, wooded slopes and steep fells, which are riddled with the abandoned workings of copper and iron ore mines. It is situated by an old pack-horse bridge, built across the beck, and contains a small number of old stone cottages, an inn and a corn mill. There has been a mill on this site since the thirteenth century, powered by the fast-flowing waters of the Whillan Beck, which races down the valley from its sources in the peaks of Scafell, the slopes of the surrounding fells and Burnmoor Tarn. Dating from the sixteenth century, the Eskdale Corn Mill was restored by Cumbria County Council and still retains its original machinery, including two water-wheels. It also houses exhibitions on farming practices and methods of milling. The tiny church of St Catherine, with its unified nave and chancel, lies half a mile south of the mill by the banks of the River Esk.

ROMAN BATH HOUSE, RAVENGLASS

From the fort of Galava at Ambleside, the Romans constructed a tortuous road right across Lakeland, over the high, savage passes of Wrynose and Hardknott, to the western coast and the port of Ravenglass, or *Glannoventa*, meaning 'the market by the shore'. Less than half a mile south of Ravenglass village, the fort served as a naval base for the whole of north-west England. Built of red sandstone in the first century AD, it was located on a cliff, facing up the Eskdale valley, near the confluence of the rivers Esk, Mite and Irt. Very little of the ancient Roman fort remains today, but a short distance away to the east, standing in a dark strip of conifer plantation, is what has been described as 'the best preserved Roman building in the north of England'. The Roman bath house, with its walls standing in parts almost 12 feet high, was about 40 feet wide and about 90 feet long, and contained everything from hot saunas to cold baths. It is preserved by English Heritage.

MUNCASTER CASTLE, RAVENGLASS

The ancestral home of the Penningtons since the thirteenth century, Muncaster Castle occupies one of the most idyllic settings in Lakeland. It is situated in beautifully landscaped gardens and parkland on the southern slopes of Muncaster Fell, one mile east of the Roman harbour at Ravenglass. The view from the Terrace Walk, described by Ruskin as the 'gateway to paradise', looks north-east up the luxuriant Esk valley to the other Lakeland fells. The castle, built of local pink granite and now essentially a Victorian country house, stands on the site of a Roman fort. The oldest part of the present building is the pele tower, erected in 1325, to which the hall and kitchens were added in the fifteenth century. Extensive alterations were carried out in the late eighteenth century and, between 1860 and 1864, a second tower was added to balance the original pele. The house and grounds are open to the public.

ST PAUL'S CHURCHYARD, IRTON

By the beginning of the seventh century AD the English had begun to colonize Cumbria from the east, establishing numerous settlements along the western coast. The churchyard of St Paul's Church at Irton contains a beautiful ninth-century example of Anglian sculpture, considered to be one of the most important in Cumbria. Standing about 10 feet high, Irton Cross, is remarkably well preserved, despite being over 1,000 years old. Its graceful, tapering shaft is intricately decorated with interlaced patterns and runic inscriptions. There is a replica of the red sandstone cross in the Lakeland Heritage Centre, Ambleside. The church itself was built in the mid-nineteenth century and stands, in peaceful isolation, on a low, green hill above the River Irt, with distant views of the Wasdale and Eskdale fells. It is located less than one mile east of Holmrook, a small village lying on the western boundary of the National Park.

ST MARY'S CHURCH, GOSFORTH

The Church of St Mary stands on the eastern outskirts of the large village of Gosforth and on the western boundary of the National Park. According to Pevsner, it possesses the 'richest haul in the county of Anglo-Saxon and Anglo-Danish work'. Its greatest and most treasured possession is the beautifully carved sandstone cross in the churchyard, which dates from the tenth century. Almost 15 feet high, the tall and extremely slender Gosforth Cross displays a fascinating fusion of Christian and pagan symbols. The rounded lower shaft is carved to represent *Yggdrasil*, the sacred ash tree in Scandinavian mythology thought to stand at the centre of the universe and support the world. The four faces of the upper, squared section depict (among other things) a biblical crucifixion and scenes illustrating the epic Edda poem, the *Voluspa*. The carvings seem to tell of the passing of the old pagan Norse gods and the coming of Christ, who conquered the forces of darkness.

ENNERDALE WATER

One of the wildest and most remote of the sixteen lakes, Ennerdale is isolated from central Lakeland by a formidable barrier of rocky peaks including Pillar, Steeple and Great Gable. It was visited by Coleridge and Wordsworth on their 'Pikteresk Toor' of the lakes in 1799, but since then it has changed dramatically. The once barren fellsides and desolate scree slopes have been transformed into a vast forest of dark green conifers, stretching for a distance of some six miles from the steep crag of Bowness Knott – halfway along the northern shore – to the head of the valley. The lake has also become a reservoir, supplying water – by means of a weir at its western end – to the towns and industries of the coast. It is a deep glacial lake, two and a half miles long and about half a mile wide reaching a maximum depth of 148 feet. The water is exceptionally clear and contains a variety of fish. It is the only lake that does not have a road running alongside it.

ENNERDALE from Cauda Brow

The village of Ennerdale Bridge lies on the western boundary of the National Park, just over a mile west of Ennerdale Water. The church of St Mary was built in 1858 on the site of an earlier chapel which had been visited by Wordsworth and Coleridge in 1799. It was here that Wordsworth heard the story of the shepherd who had fallen asleep upon the top of Pillar and plunged to his death, the incident which inspired him to write his poem *The Brothers*. Steeple, Pillar and Great Gable are among the magnificent peaks which dominate the head of the valley, where the River Liza winds for five long miles – through a dark forest of conifers – before entering the lake. The stream that emerges from the foot of Ennerdale Water is the River Ehen, which eventually enters the sea near British Nuclear Fuels' power station at Sellafield.

WASDALE
from Westmorland Cairn, Great Gable

Just over 100 yards from the summit of Great Gable – 2,949 feet above sea-level – Westmorland Cairn, stands on the edge of a precipice, from which there is a breathtaking view south-west, looking down into and along the deep glacier-gouged valley of Wasdale. Lingmell Beck can be clearly seen snaking its way down the dale – through lush, green pastures, divided by a network of dry-stone walls – to Wastwater. The lake is three miles long, half a mile wide and extremely deep, at 258 feet the deepest in Lakeland. It is also the most dramatic of all the lakes, with an immense wall of screes plunging deep into its waters on the south-eastern side. The River Irt issues from the foot of the lake and falls into the estuary of the River Esk at Ravenglass, before entering the Irish Sea. The water in Wastwater itself is pure and clear but, because it is not rich in nutrients, it can only support fish like char and trout. It is used as a reservoir by British Nuclear Fuels.

GREAT GABLE
from Wastwater

'When people go forth to see the world,' wrote Thomas Wilkinson, 'they are sometimes in search of beauty. If beauty is the leading object of their search, they need not go to Wast Water. The prominent features round Wast Water are sternness and sterility. . . . The mountains of Wast Water are naked to their base: – their sides and their summits are uniform: their summits shoot up into lofty points, and end in the form of pyramids.' Viewed from the shores of Wastwater, Great Gable does indeed appear as a pyramid; rugged and distinctive, standing alone and aloof from its lofty neighbours. Although at 2,949 feet it is 261 feet lower than Scafell Pike, it dominates the dale-head, and fittingly, this view of Great Gable from Wastwater has become the official emblem of the National Park. (Great Gable is in the centre of the photograph; Yewbarrow is on the left; and Lingmell and Scafell are on the right).

ST OLAF'S CHURCH, WASDALE HEAD

The tiny, long, low church of St Olaf at Wasdale Head is surrounded by some of the grandest mountains in Lakeland, including Scafell Pike, Great End and Great Gable. Reached by a long road running along the western edge of Wastwater, the church and its graveyard are almost hidden by yew trees and can be easily missed. Although the age of the church is not known, it is considered to be at least 400 years old and is probably older. In 1976 the original church register was discovered, and found to contain records dating back to 1620. But the earliest reference to the church at Wasdale Head was made in the middle of the sixteenth century, when the Bishop of Chester demanded a contribution from the parish towards the upkeep of St Bees Priory Church. In 1979 it was decided that the little church, which previously had no name, should be dedicated to St Olaf, after the Norse king, who was converted to Christianity and later became a saint.

ST OLAF'S CHURCH, WASDALE HEAD

There is a much-quoted saying about Wasdale Head that the parish contains England's highest mountain, deepest lake, smallest church and biggest liar! The mountain is Scafell Pike and the lake is Wastwater. The claim, however, that the church is England's smallest was investigated by Raymond F. Bowers, rector of the parish, who concluded that the smallest was really St Edwold's at Stockwood in Dorset. But, because it was no longer in use, he decided that St Beuno's at Culbone in Somerset should 'stand in the number one spot'. However, he argued that in any account of size, cubic capacity should be considered: and, if that is the case, then the tiny stone church at Wasdale Head is indeed the smallest! It is 35 feet 9 inches in length, 14 feet 2 inches in width and the walls stand only 6 feet 6 inches high. The parish's claim to possession of the biggest liar arose at the end of the nineteenth century when Will Ritson, the innkeeper at the Wasdale Head Inn, was given the title.

81
78

WASTWATER SCREES, WASTWATER

'A sheet of water between 3 and 4 miles in length,' wrote Coleridge of Wastwater in his 1802 *Tour of the Lake Country*, 'the whole or very nearly the whole of its right Bank formed by Screes . . . or Shiver, consisting of fine red Streaks running in broad Stripes thro' a stone colour – slanting off from the Perpendicular, as steep as the meal newly ground from the Miller's spout . . . like a pointed Decanter in shape, or an out-spread Fan, or a long-waisted old maid with a fine prim Apron. . . .' Wastwater Screes – consisting of millions of fragments of broken and crumbling rock, some of considerable size – rise almost 2,000 feet from the floor of the lake to the rugged crags of Illgill Head. Dominating the south-eastern side of the lake, they form a spectacular wall of sloping rubble, constantly varying in mood and colour with the changing weather and the seasons.

SCAFELL AND LINGMELL from Wastwater

Rising above Wastwater are Scafell Pike (3,210 feet) in the centre, Scafell (3,162 feet) on the right and seemingly higher, and Lingmell (2,649) on the left. The scattered hamlet of Wasdale Head – with its tiny church, hotel, stone cottages and farmsteads – lies at the north-eastern end of Wastwater in spectacularly beautiful surroundings. It has long been a popular centre for climbers and walkers, who gather in the bar of the Wasdale Head Inn, not only to exchange stories but also – according to tradition – to tell the 'biggest of lies'. From Wasdale Head a pack-horse track climbs up the Lingmell Beck valley to Borrowdale and Great Langdale, via the 1,600-foot-high Sty Head Pass. The shortest and most usual route to the top of Scafell Pike also starts from Wasdale Head – a route taking on average three hours up and two hours down.

BUTTERMERE & THE NORTH-WESTERN LAKES

BUTTERMERE VILLAGE, BUTTERMERE

Buttermere village lies between Buttermere and Crummock Water and is surrounded by high fells and some of the wildest and prettiest scenery in the Lakes. The tiny church of St James (built in 1840) stands on elevated ground above two inns and a cluster of stone-built cottages on the steep winding road to Newlands Hause and Newlands Valley. This is one of only two roads to Buttermere from Keswick, both leading over high passes (Newlands and Honister) that for centuries protected the valley from invasion. The village made national news in 1802 when it was discovered that one of the villagers, Mary Robinson, had been tricked into marriage by a man calling himself the Hon. Augustus Hope. He turned out to be a rogue, an imposter and a bigamist. Her story became the subject for several plays and books and she passed into popular legend as the Maid of Buttermere.

'The Grasmere Sports', wrote Canon Rawnsley in 1899, 'are to the dalesman of Westmorland and Cumberland what the gathering for the Highland games is to men across the Border.' Although many of the national sports have been popular in Lakeland for centuries, there are three sports which are special to the area, wrestling, fell-racing and hound trailing, and a fourth which tends to dominate the dalesman's way of life, fox hunting. The sheep-farmers of Lakeland have always argued that fox hunting is essential, for the large numbers of foxes roaming the fells have to be checked to protect their livestock and therefore, ultimately, their livelihood.

At first, individual farmers set traps and snares to try and reduce the fox population but, as the numbers of foxes increased, they banded together to form packs of specially bred hounds. There are six packs in the region: the Blencathra, which hunts the northern fells around Keswick; the Ullswater, whose territory is the fells around Patterdale and Mardale; the Lunesdale, which hunts a wide area of the eastern fells outside the National Park; the Coniston, which hunts Langdale, the Old Man, the Furness Fells and southern Lakeland; the Eskdale and Ennerdale, which hunts the wild, rough western fells, including Pillar and Scafell; and the Melbreak, whose territory is the north-western fells around Buttermere, Loweswater and Lorton.

Fox hunting in Lakeland, however, is unlike the fashionable sport found in the rest of England, for the terrain is far too rough for horses, and thus the hunters are given no option but to follow the hounds on foot. During the season, from the beginning of September to the end of April, hunting will go on in all kinds of weather and it requires strong legs and stamina to keep up with the fox, which often makes for the tops of the fells when pursued. Only the huntsman wears the traditional scarlet coat, although it is thought that the legendary John Peel, who hunted the fells 'back o' Skidda', wore not a 'coat so gay' but a 'coat so gray'.

Traditional Cumberland and Westmorland wrestling is an extremely popular local sport with championships taking place in many of Lakeland's summer shows and fairs. Although the origin of the sport is unknown, some authorities believe that it was introduced by the Norse invaders who settled in the region during the ninth and tenth centuries. It was mentioned in the sixteenth century and seems to have become organized towards the end of the eighteenth. One of the earliest recorded contests was held in 1785 on the frozen ice of Windermere, with refreshments and music supplied.

The rules of Cumberland and Westmorland wrestling are simple. The two contestants – wearing a vest and white tights with embroidered pants over them – stand face to face, with their arms locked behind each other's back and attempt to throw their opponent to the ground. If both men fall together, the winner is the man who then manoeuvres himself on top. If one man breaks his hold, or if any part of his body touches the ground except his feet, he loses the round. It is a contest not just of physical strength, but also of skill, balance, agility, patience and concentration. But Cumberland and Westmorland wrestling is essentially a sport for the wrestler, not the spectator. It is often jokingly said that if you want to appreciate the wrestling you have to enter for it.

Fell races, or guides' races as they are sometimes called, are to many people the principal attraction of the local shows and sports meetings. The course is marked by one or two flags placed high on the summit of a convenient fell near the showground. For the competitors who take part in this tough and spectacular race, the object is to run up the steep fellside, go round the flags and – descending at breakneck speed – return to the arena in the fastest time.

During the spring and summer, when fox hunting is out of season, the dalesman turns his attention to the betting sport of hound trailing, which is basically fox hunting without the fox. Prior to 1906, when the Hound Trailing Association was formed, the sport was open to all kinds of roguery and corruption, with hounds being lured away from the scent, drugged, substituted and even kidnapped. The laying of trails is now carefully supervised by H.T.A. rules and the opportunities for cheating have been virtually eliminated.

The scent is laid over a ten-mile circular course, which starts and finishes at the same point, and covers a variety of terrain, chosen to make the trail as difficult as possible. As soon as the trailers return to the starting point – having dragged a cloth soaked in aniseed and oil over the fellside – the hounds are released and they disappear into the hills. It takes them about thirty minutes to complete the course and, when the returning animals are sighted, their owners shout, whistle and scream, all willing their hounds to win.

THE SUMMIT TARN, HAYSTACKS

Standing between the head of Ennerdale and the deep trough of Warnscale Bottom, Haystacks (1,900 feet) fails to qualify for inclusion in Wainwright's 'best half-dozen' fells because of its 'inferior height'. But what it lacks in height, it makes up for in beauty and variety: rocky peaks, slippery screes, bold crags, steep gullies, precipitous cliffs, running becks, dark peat bogs and numerous tarns. Haystacks has all of these, as well as magnificent views of the lofty fells which surround it: Great Gable, Kirk Fell, Pillar, High Crag, Robinson, Fleetwith Pike, Grey Knotts and Brandreth. However, the summit of Haystacks does qualify, in Wainwright's opinion, as 'the best fell-top of all – a place of great charm and fairyland attractiveness'. It consists of a low ridge of rock, 50 yards long, with a cairn at each end and a small tarn alongside. The view from the summit takes in most of the high mountains within a five-mile radius as well as Ennerdale Water, Crummock Water and Buttermere.

SOUR MILK GILL,
BUTTERMERE VALLEY

Between the summits of High Stile and Red Pike is a small hanging valley in the middle of which lies Bleaberry Tarn, a dark oval-shaped pool. The stream that spills from the tarn, cascading about 700 feet down the steep fellside into Buttermere, is known as Sour Milk Gill. There are a number of mountain streams in Lakeland which bear this name and it seems to refer to the white foam that is created when fast-flowing water tumbles over rocks, especially after heavy rain. The long, ribbon-like strands that fall from the heights opposite Buttermere village pour down the rocky slopes through Burtness Wood, where the National Trust is gradually felling the larch and replanting with the native oak. The larch, which loses its needles in winter, was introduced into Lakeland towards the end of the eighteenth century. Wordsworth disliked it intensely, commenting in his *Guide to the Lakes* that, 'if ten thousand of this spiky tree, the larch, are stuck in at once upon the side of a hill, they can grow up into nothing but deformity.'

BUTTERMERE
from Gatesgarth

Buttermere is derived from the Old English words *butere* and *mere*, meaning 'the lake by the dairy pastures'. There is a footpath running around the perimeter of the lake – a distance of about three and a half miles – which, apart from a slight deviation at each end, keeps close to the shore. From Buttermere village the path leads south in an anti-clockwise direction across meadows to Sour Milk Gill, after which it climbs into Burtness Wood. Beyond the wood the footpath crosses Comb Beck and continues past a small mixed plantation of conifers and oaks towards Warnscale Bottom. Leaving the shore at the head of the lake, it skirts through flat farmland and crosses the Warnscale Beck to Gatesgarth, where it joins the Honister–Buttermere road. A short distance along the road – now returning to the village – the path leads back to the shore and, near Hassness, enters a short tunnel. It is said that the landowner, hating to see his gardeners idle in wet weather, set them to work on carving it out of the solid rock.

HAYSTACKS
from Buttermere

Set in a bowl of soaring fells, Buttermere – with its lush pastures and wooded shores – is a Lakeland gem. Not much bigger than neighbouring Loweswater, it is one and a quarter miles long, less than half a mile wide and over 90 feet deep. It is a clear lake, containing perch, pike, trout and char, and is fed by numerous streams. But its main feeder is Gatesgarthdale Beck, which carries sediment – washed down from the green slate quarries on Honister Crag – from Honister Pass down the valley to deposit it in the lake, a factor that probably accounts for the greenish tinge of the water. At the head of the lake – rising from the deep hollow of Warnscale Bottom near Gatesgarth – is Haystacks (shown in the photograph), its great wall of dark crags resembling a stack of hay in a field. Although it is less than 2,000 feet high and is, therefore, lower than its loftier neighbours, it is the one fell (out of all the fells in Lakeland) chosen by Wainwright to receive his ashes.

HONISTER QUARRY,
HONISTER CRAG

High above Honister Pass on the awesome cliffs of Honister Crag are several entrances to a vast labyrinth of tunnels that lead right into the heart of the rock at different levels. The crag has been industrially quarried for its attractive green volcanic slate since at least 1643. Conditions for the quarrymen were both primitive and dangerous, and right up until the beginning of the twentieth century they were expected to work by candlelight. Accidents were frequent, hours were long and wages were low. But, despite the fact that some were worn out by the effort of their labour, others managed to perform feats that by today's standards seem staggering. Joseph Clarke, it is said, managed in one day to bring down over five tons of slate from the quarry in less than seventeen journeys. The photograph was taken at the Road End entrance of the quarry, which is now closed. The 2-foot-wide rails once carried trucks into and out of the tunnels, while the cabins were used for rest and shelter.

HONISTER CRAG
from Honister Hause

Honister Hause, 1,190 feet above sea-level, is a watershed between the mountain streams that flow north-westwards into Buttermere and Crummock Water to form the River Cocker and those that flow eastwards to form the River Derwent. Honister Crag, part of the volcanic fell of Fleetwith, is a well-known landmark which towers dramatically above the boulder-strewn pass linking Borrowdale to Buttermere. It extends north-westwards for two miles from the top of Honister Pass to Gatesgarth and is scarred by natural debris and spoil from centuries of green slate quarrying. Honister quarry has been in production since the mid-seventeenth century and, although the underground levels are now closed, slate continues to be extracted by open-top quarrying. The finest quality slate was located near the top of the crag and, before the introduction of gravitational railways in the late nineteenth century, the quarrymen had to manoeuvre the stone down the steep fellside in sledges.

BUTTERMERE VALLEY
from Fleetwith Pike

During the nineteenth century and the early part of the twentieth century there were daily tours in the summer months from Keswick to Buttermere, known as the Buttermere Round. The route, which was extremely popular, went through Borrowdale, over Honister Pass to Buttermere, and returned by way of Newlands Hause to Keswick. The twenty-two-mile round-trip was made in horse-drawn carriages and, whenever the road became too steep for the horses to climb with a full load, the passengers had to get out and walk. Between Seatoller, in Borrowdale, and the slate quarries at the top of Honister Hause the quarrymen constructed a road with less of a gradient than the old one, and, for the payment of a toll, the ascent of the pass was made easier. The view north-westwards down the Buttermere valley from Fleetwith Pike includes Buttermere and Crummock Water.

WORDSWORTH HOUSE, COCKERMOUTH

In *The Prelude* Wordsworth recollected his 'sweet Birthplace': he described the 'ceaseless music' of the Derwent and how, having left the mountains,

> . . . to the Towers
> Of Cockermouth that beauteous River came,
> Behind my Father's House he pass'd, close by,
> Along the margin of our Terrace Walk.

The 'fairest of all rivers' still runs behind this apricot-coloured Georgian house. It belonged to Sir James Lowther, who let it to his agent, John Wordsworth, the poet's father. Wordsworth was born at the house on the 7 April 1770, the second eldest in a family of five. Dorothy, his sister, was born on Christmas Day the following year. Richard, the eldest, was born in 1768, John was born in 1772 and Christopher in 1774. Their mother, Ann (*née* Cookson), died in 1778 when William was only eight years old, and the children were sent to stay with relatives.

WORDSWORTH HOUSE, COCKERMOUTH

Wordsworth House, situated at the western end of Main Street, is described by Pevsner as 'quite a swagger house for such a town', with eight large casement windows on the ground floor and a porch with Tuscan columns. The house was built in 1745 and was purchased by Sir James Lowther in 1764. Two years later, after their marriage, the poet's parents moved into the house. In 1938, when the house was threatened with demolition, it was bought by a public appeal and given to the National Trust. It is open to the public and still retains many of its original features. The library (shown in the photograph) contains two items of furniture which belonged to Wordsworth: a large painted bookcase brought from Rydal Mount and a bureau-bookcase presented to the Trust by the poet's great-granddaughter. In the rest of the house there are some fine pieces of period furniture, paintings, portraits and china.

DRY-STONE WALL, LOWESWATER

One of the most distinctive features of Lakeland are the dry-stone walls. Although they appear to be ancient, most of the walls were built in the eighteenth and nineteenth centuries, particularly after the Enclosure Act of 1801, when the majority of the open fells and commons became private property. Some dry-stone walls, however, are considerably older, dating back at least seven hundred years. These ancient and sometimes massive structures were mainly constructed to delineate the boundaries of parishes, estates and manors. But dry-stone walls were not just built as boundaries: they provide shelter for sheep; they prevent the animals from straying over precipices; they form sheep pens; and they also serve as places to put stones. In order to create pasture-land the ground had to be cleared of stones, and these were used in the building of walls. Those that were surplus were piled in great heaps, known as 'clearance cairns'.

LOWESWATER

Just over a mile long, half a mile broad and reaching a maximum depth of 60 feet, this gentle, secretive lake is unique, for it is the only one whose waters flow inwards towards the centre of Lakeland. Its outlet, Park Beck, flows in a south-easterly direction before it empties into Crummock Water. Between these two lakes is Loweswater village, situated in the middle of a flat, fertile alluvial plain similar to the one which divides Crummock Water from Buttermere. It is possible that all three of these lakes were once joined together, filling the Buttermere valley with water. Loweswater means 'leafy lake' and – running down to its south-eastern shore – is Holme Wood, a beautiful mile-long strip of mixed woodland, with conifers on the higher slopes of the fellside and oak, ash, alder, elm and birch below. Hidden amongst the trees is also a small waterfall, Holme Force. The fell in the centre of the photograph is Grasmoor, the 2,791-foot-high mass that towers over Crummock Water.

LOWESWATER

The three lakes of Buttermere, Crummock Water and Loweswater lie entirely in Skiddaw Slate, the oldest rock in Lakeland and one of the oldest in the world. It is an ancient mud rock that breaks easily into small fragments to form screes (like those on the steep north-eastern slope of Mellbreak), eventually becoming soil on which grass and heather grows. The area is noted for its rich variety of wild life; from woodland and lakeland plants and insects to mountain and moorland birds and animals. The Melbreak, one of the National Park's five fox hunting packs, hunts the fells around Buttermere and Loweswater on foot, often meeting outside the Kirkstile Inn in the village of Loweswater. From the wooded southern shore of Loweswater five fells fan out like the fingers of a giant hand: Burnbank Fell, Blake Fell, Gavel Fell, Hen Comb and Mellbreak, the distinctive fell that dominates Crummock Water.

CRUMMOCK WATER, BUTTERMERE VALLEY

Once one large lake, Buttermere and Crummock Water are now separated by a narrow half-mile strip of land. Crummock Water is the larger of the two, almost double the size of Buttermere, measuring two and a half miles long, over half a mile wide and 144 feet deep. It is a clear rocky-bottomed lake flanked by steep fellsides of Skiddaw slate: to the east, the bracken-covered slopes of Grasmoor and Whiteless Pike, and to the west, the bare scree slopes of Mellbreak. The red squirrel can be found high up on the northern shore of the lake, in Lanthwaite Wood. The lake is fed by numerous streams, including the beck from Scale Force which – with a single drop of 172 feet – is the biggest waterfall in Lakeland. Near where the lake receives the Park Beck from Loweswater the water flows northwards over a weir to become the River Cocker. The distant range of fells in the photograph is the High Stile range dividing Ennerdale from the Buttermere valley.

VALE OF LORTON
from near Hullary Wood

From Crummock Water, the River Cocker flows north through the green and fertile Vale of Lorton to Cockermouth, where it is joined by the River Derwent. The village of Lorton is situated in the middle of the vale, near where the road from Buttermere to Cockermouth meets the road over Whinlatter Pass. It is divided into two: Low Lorton, standing on the banks of the River Cocker, and High Lorton, located on higher ground just over half a mile to the east. Lorton Hall, in Low Lorton, is a historic manor house, built mainly in the seventeenth century around a defensive medieval pele tower. In 1804 Wordsworth and Dorothy travelled over Whinlatter Pass to visit, in his sister's words, 'a Yew tree which is the Patriarch of Yew trees, green and flourishing, in very old age – the largest tree I ever saw.' The tree, the 'pride of Lorton Vale', was immortalized by Wordsworth in his poem *Yew-Trees*. Although ancient and decayed, it still stands in High Lorton.

HIGHLAND CATTLE,
CRUMMOCK WATER

Until the arrival of the railways in the middle of the nineteenth century, long, slow-moving lines of cattle – on their way to fresh pastures or to one of the great cattle fairs of the district – were a familiar sight in Lakeland. Vast herds of animals, numbering in thousands, made the journey south from Scotland into Cumbria, and many Cumbrians travelled north to attend the great cattle fairs held across the border. The trade in cattle between Scotland and the north of England dates back to the mid-fourteenth century and probably earlier. In his story *The Two Drovers* Walter Scott describes one of these journeys into Cumbria. Among the beasts introduced into Lakeland from Scotland were the wild-looking Highland cattle, with their long, sweeping horns and shaggy coats. The hardiest breed of cattle in Britain, they are able, with their thick, doubly-insulated coats, to remain outside throughout the winter.

Photographic notes

For one year I photographed this most beautiful area of England and soon began to appreciate that taking pictures of the English Lakes could become a way of life. The region is so incredibly photogenic, with the lakes, valleys and mountains offering a variety of landscapes, and the changeable weather a mood for each day. The problem for a photographer is just where to point the camera best to depict each place and to do justice to it pictorially.

A definite plan was essential so that the maximum could be obtained from each day: but each plan had to be flexible to allow for alternatives, in case the weather changed for the worse (which it frequently did).

Photography from the fells was made easier by good visibility over many miles, but there were very few days that offered this clarity. In fact, when the weather seemed ideal at the bottom of a mountain it could soon deteriorate and become positively dangerous. Suitable equipment for walking and a lot of common sense were essential. My days on the mountains were trouble-free and reasonably productive – although all the fells I photographed were visited at least twice, and some many times more to achieve the right conditions.

The lakes and rivers were perhaps my favourite aspects of Lakeland, each one being quite different and offering its own particular character.

Autumn and winter, early mornings and late evenings were certainly the best times for photography. The mists on the water and in the valleys, and the changing colours of the landscape were a joy to experience, and also presented excellent photographic opportunities.

The properties were a pleasant change from the landscapes and some of their gardens were very photogenic. After some initial research (to discover the best part of the year, time of day, type of light and so on) the photographs were easily taken. The interiors required careful planning and were lit with short duration flash simply to fill out the heavy shadows within the rooms.

From the beginning of the project I decided to use the largest film format practical (larger sizes offering greater recording ability) and opted to use the Pentax 6 × 7, a camera which, despite being heavy, is very rugged and fast to use. Lenses were 55mm, 75mm and 200mm. Only occasionally did I use 35mm equipment, which consisted of a Nikon F3 with 24mm and 35mm lenses. 81A warming filters were used frequently and a polariser and graduated grey sparingly; no other filters were used. As always the trusty medium-weight Gitzo tripod went everywhere. The film I used was Fuji 50 and 100 and all equipment was carried in a standard rucksack.

Rob Talbot

Selected properties

THE NATIONAL TRUST

Regional Office
The National Trust
Rothay Holme, Rothay Road,
Ambleside, Cumbria, LA22 0EJ
Telephone: (05394) 33883

Hill Top
Near Sawrey, Hawkshead, Cumbria,
LA22 0LF
Telephone: (09666) 269
Open: Easter to end October except Thursdays and Fridays

Sizergh Castle
Kendal, Cumbria, LA8 8EZ
Telephone: (05395) 60070
Open: Easter to October except Tuesdays, Fridays and Saturdays

Townend
Troutbeck, Windermere, Cumbria,
LA23 1LB
Telephone: (05394) 32628
Open: Easter to end October except Mondays and Saturdays

Wordsworth House
The Main Street, Cockermouth, Cumbria,
CA13 9RX
Telephone: (0900) 824805
Open: April to end October except Thursdays

MISCELLANEOUS

Brantwood
Coniston, Cumbria, LA21 8AD
Telephone: (0966) 41396
Open: March to November

Brockhole Visitor Centre
Windermere, Cumbria, LA23 1LJ
Telephone: (09662) 6601
Open: March to early November

Dalemain Mansion & Gardens
Stainton, Penrith, Cumbria, CA11 0HB
Telephone: (08536) 450
Open: Easter to mid-October except Fridays and Saturdays

Dove Cottage
The Wordsworth Trust, Grasmere,
Cumbria, LA22 9SH
Telephone: (09665) 544 & 547
Open: Throughout the year

Eskdale Corn Mill
Boot, Cumbria, CA19 1TG
Telephone: (09403) 335
Open: March to September (closed every Saturday except Bank Holidays)

Hawkshead Grammar School
Main Street, Hawkshead, Cumbria
Open: Easter to October except Wednesdays

Levens Hall
Kendal, Cumbria, LA8 0PD
Telephone: (05395) 60321
Open: Easter to end September except Fridays and Saturdays

Mirehouse
Keswick, Cumbria, CA12 4QE
Telephone: (0596) 72287
Open: April to October on Sundays, Wednesdays, Bank Holiday Monday afternoons and other times by appointment

Muncaster Castle
Ravenglass, West Cumbria, CA18 1RQ
Telephone: (0657 7) 614 & 203
Open: April to September except Mondays

Rydal Mount
Ambleside, Cumbria, LA22 9LU
Telephone: (05394) 33002
Open: Throughout the year

Bibliography

Baddeley, M. J. B., *The English Lake District*, 1902
Bailey, Brian J., *Lakeland Walks and Legends*, Granada, 1981
Barringer, Chris, *National Trust Histories: The Lake District*, Willow, 1984
Bateson, F. W., *Wordsworth, a Re-Interpretation*, Longman, 1954
Berry, Geoffrey, & Beard, Geoffrey, *The Lake District A Century of Conservation*, Bartholomew, 1980
Bodman, Janet, *Lake District Stone Walls*, Dalesman, 1984
Boyes, Malcolm, *Exploring the Lake District*, Dalesman, 1984
Bradley, A. G., *Highways and Byways in the Lake District*, Macmillan, 1901
Bragg, Melvyn, *Land of the Lakes*, Secker & Warburg, 1983
Clare, T., *Archaeological Sites of the Lake District*, Moorland, 1981
Clark, Geoffrey, & Thompson, W. Harding, *The Lakeland Landscape*, Black, 1938
Clark, Kenneth, *Ruskin Today*, Penguin, 1982
Coburn, Kathleen, *In Pursuit of Coleridge*, Bodley Head, 1977
Coburn, Kathleen (ed.), *Notebooks of S. T. Coleridge*, Routledge & Kegan Paul, 1962–74
Coleridge, Samuel Taylor, *Biographia Literaria*, 1817
Collingwood, W. G., *The Lake Counties*, Dent, 1932
Countryside Commission (ed.), *Lake District: National Park Guide No. 6*, H.M.S.O., 1969
Cumberland Geological Society, *The Lake District*, Unwin, 1982
Davies, Hunter, *A Walk Around the Lakes*, Weidenfeld, 1979
Davies, Hunter, *The Good Guide to the Lakes*, Forster Davies, 1984
De Quincey, Thomas, *Recollections of the Lake Poets*, Penguin, 1970
Dunn, Michael, *The Lake District*, David & Charles, 1988
Eyre, Kathleen, *Famous Lakeland Homes*, Dalesman, 1975
Findler, Gerald, *Folk Lore of the Lake Counties*, Dalesman, 1968
Findler, Gerald, *Ghosts of the Lake Counties*, Dalesman, 1969
Findler, Gerald, *Lakeland Legends*, Dalesman, 1984
FitzGibbon, Mary Rose, *Lakeland Scene*, Chapman & Hall, 1948
Fraser, Maxwell, *Companion into Lakeland*, Methuen, 1937
Gambles, Robert, *Lake District Place-Names*, Dalesman, 1985
Gambles, Robert, *Man in Lakeland*, Dalesman, 1975
Garlick, Tom, *Romans in the Lake Counties*, Dalesman, 1970
Gilpin, William, *Observations Relative Chiefly to the Picturesque Beauty Made in the Year 1772 in Several Parts of England, Particularly the Mountains and Lakes of Cumberland and Westmorland*, 1786
Goddard, Frank, *Lakeland Fells*, Dalesman, 1975
Griffin, A. H., *Inside the Real Lakeland*, Guardian, 1961
Holland, Eric G., *Coniston Copper Mines: A Field Guide*, Cicerone, 1981
Hutchinson, Thomas (ed.), *The Poetical Works of Wordsworth*, O.U.P., 1932
Hutchinson, William, *An Excursion to the Lakes in Westmorland and Cumberland in 1773 and 1774*, 1776
Lane, Margaret, *The Magic Years of Beatrix Potter*, Warne, 1978
Lane, Margaret, *The Tale of Beatrix Potter*, Warne, 1968
Lefebure, Molly, *Cumberland Heritage*, Gollancz, 1970
Lefebure, Molly, *The English Lake District*, Batsford, 1964
Lefebure, Molly, *The Illustrated Lake Poets*, Windward, 1987
Ludlum, Stuart D. (ed.), *Exploring The Lake District 100 Years Ago*, Thames & Hudson, 1985
Marsh, Terry, *The Lake Mountains: One & Two*, Hodder & Stoughton, 1987
Marshall, J. D., *Old Lakeland*, David & Charles, 1971
Martineau, Harriet, *Complete Guide to the Lakes*, 1855
Matthews, Bob, *Lakeland's Literary Heritage*, Jarrold, 1985
McCracken, David, *Wordsworth & The Lake District*, O.U.P., 1984
McFadzean, Alen, *Wythburn Mine and the Lead Miners of Helvellyn*, Red Earth, 1987
Mc.Intire, Walter T., *Lakeland and the Borders of Long Ago*, Cumberland News, 1948
Mee, Arthur, *Lake Counties*, Hodder & Stoughton, 1937
Miers, Richenda, *Cumbria*, Cadogan, 1986
Mitchell, W. R., *Lake District Sports*, Dalesman, 1977
Mitchell, W. R. (intro.), *The Lake Poets*, Dalesman, 1980
Nicholson, Norman, *The Lake District: an Anthology*, Hale, 1977
Nicholson, Norman, *Portrait of the Lakes*, Hale, 1963
Parker, John, *Lake District*, Warne, 1978
Pevsner, Nikolaus, *Cumberland and Westmorland*, (Buildings of England Series) Penguin, 1967
Poucher, W. A., *Lakeland Fells*, Constable, 1985
Poucher, W. A., *The Lake District*, Constable, 1982
Powell, Richard & Wood, Donna (eds.), *Ordnance Survey Leisure Guide to the Lake District*, Automobile Association & Ordnance Survey, 1984
Raistrick, Arthur, *Faces of Lakeland*, Peters, 1987
Rawnsley, H. D., *Reminiscences of Wordsworth among the Peasantry of Westmorland*, 1882
Rollinson, William, *A History of Cumberland and Westmorland*, Phillimore, 1978
Rollinson, William, *Life and Tradition in the Lake District*, Dent, 1974
Sands, Ronald, *A Portrait of Wordsworth Country*, Hale, 1984

Sands, Ronald (comp.), *Poetry of Lakeland*, Peters, 1985
Sands, Ronald, *William Wordsworth*, Pitkin, 1981
Scott, Daniel, *Cumberland and Westmorland*, Methuen, 1920
Singleton, Frank, *The English Lakes*, Batsford, 1954
Slack, Margaret, *Lakeland Discovered: From No Man's Land to National Park*, Hale, 1982
Taylor, Roland, *The Lake District*, Geographia, n.d.
Thornton, Peter, *Lakeland from the Air*, Dalesman, 1985
Victoria and Albert Museum, *The Discovery of the Lake District*, V & A, 1984
Wainwright, A., *A Pictorial Guide to the Lakeland Fells: Books One to Seven*, Westmorland Gazette, 1955–1966
Wainwright, A., *Coast to Coast Walk*, Michael Joseph, 1987
Wainwright, A., *Fellwalking with Wainwright*, Michael Joseph, 1984
Walpole, Sir Hugh, *Herries Chronicle*, Pan, 1971
Ward Lock, *Guide to the English Lakes*, 1891
West, Thomas, *A Guide to the Lakes*, 1780
Wordsworth, Dorothy, *Illustrated Lakeland Journals*, Collins, 1987
Wordsworth Jonathan, *William and Dorothy, The Dove Cottage Years 1799–1808*, Wordsworth Trust, 1987
Wordsworth, William, *A Guide through the District of the Lakes in the North of England* . . . (5th edition), 1835
Wyatt, John, *The Lake District National Park*, Webb & Bower, 1987

Index

Numbers in *italics* refer to illustrations